SYNERGIZATION

Unlocking Stability, Potential,
Progress, and Achievement

David S. Philemon

Royal Diadem Publishing Inc.

Dedication

To the Almighty God, my Rock, Refuge, and Source of all wisdom and strength. Thank You for Your unwavering love, grace, and the purpose You've placed within me. May this book bring glory to Your name and draw others closer to You.

And to my beloved spiritual parents, Dr. Paul and Dr. Mrs. Becky Paul Enenche, who have faithfully nurtured and guided me in this journey. Your example of unwavering devotion, godly counsel, and compassionate care has been a beacon of light and strength in my life. Thank you for standing as pillars of faith and for your steadfast commitment to the Kingdom.

CONTENTS

ACKNOWLEDGMENTS

This book would not have been possible without the unwavering support, dedication, and talent of an extraordinary team. My deepest gratitude goes to each of you for your contributions, insights, and encouragement throughout this journey.

First and foremost, thank you to Rev. Mimi Philemon my dear wife, Rev. Shina Gentry, and and my assistant pastor Rev. Bright Amudoaghan for your incredible effort, encouragement, and belief in this project. Your support has been instrumental in bringing this vision to life.

To the dedicated leaders of Royal Diadem Publishing, Ide Imogie and Kishawna Bailey, I am immensely grateful for your belief in this project from the very beginning and for investing your time and energy into its development. Your creativity, dedication, and expertise have been the backbone of this endeavor.

I am especially grateful to the Royal Diadem Publishing team— Beulah Orogun, Emmanuella Ben-Eboh, Doyinsade Awodele, Kim Matthews, and Shante Gill, for your meticulous attention to detail, refining every page and ensuring that each word reflects our vision.

A heartfelt thank you to my family, friends, and colleagues whose unwavering support and belief in this project gave me the courage and strength to see it through.

Finally, thank you to all the readers and supporters who make this work meaningful. I am humbled and honored to share this journey with each of you.

With all my gratitude,
David Philemon

INTRODUCTION

One of the greatest mysteries that come with our human existence as ordained by God is that we are not meant to survive on our own, and this is a revelation that many Christians often overlook and that's why they are always defeated by the challenges of life and are often devoured as prey by the devil and his demonic agents. When you begin to understand that you are never meant to live by your strength alone then you have caught the key to unlocking unimaginable dimensions of power, potential, ability, and authority in your life. I want you to understand that we as men are beings of power and authority who originated from God, but that isn't all, we also have what we call our "mystical union with God", this mystical union is the fact that "God is in us, and We are in God" it's a two-way dimensional reality that is absolutely necessary to understand if you want to truly walk in the power that is available to us as children of God. Oh my God! Can you feel the weight of that truth? This is the power of "synergization" that I am talking about. It is a revelation that will revolutionize your understanding of your relationship with God and your potential in Him.

Have you ever read the book of John 15:4-5? This scripture beautifully explains synergization for us by saying "Abide in me, and I in you. As the branch cannot bear fruit of itself, except it abide in the vine; no more can ye, except ye abide in me. I am the vine, ye are the branches: He that abideth in me, and I in him, the same bringeth forth much fruit: for without me ye can do nothing." Can you see it? We are not just in God; God is also in us. It is a divine synergy that creates a power greater than anything we could muster on our own, and just in case you are not fully getting the magnitude of this truth, let me show you another amazing scripture that also explains it. 1 John 4:13 says, "Hereby know we that we dwell in him, and he in us, because he hath given us of his Spirit." I tell you the truth, there is great power within you, and nothing can defeat you when you understand the Power of "synergization" - first by synergizing with God, the ultimate of all synergies, and then by synergizing with other men, agents, systems, organizations, heavenly beings and angelic hosts that the Lord has ordained to walk with you in life.

If there is one thing you must know and I want you to never forget it in your life, it is the fact that human strength is greatly limited, no matter how great you are as an individual, you have your own limitations but through synergization you can be sure of stability, progress, and achievement. Even in our spiritual lives, we are not meant to be lone rangers in the Kingdom of God, we are meant to be part of a body with each member synergizing with the others to create a force that can shake the very gates of hell. This is why the enemy works so hard to keep us isolated, divided, and segregated in the body of Christ, he knows that without synergization we are vulnerable.

This is not just a fancy theory, it is a revelation straight from the throne of Grace, a divine strategy through which God intends to elevate both you as an individual and the entire body of Christ to the next level. As you read further into this truth, I want you to know that God is speaking to you directly, He is not just imparting knowledge, He is set to bring establishment into your life, and just in case the devil has been bastardizing you, trying to make you feel small and insignificant, I also want you to know that his reign has come to an end in your life today as you begin to understand "synergization" in the mighty name of Jesus.

This is your time!

This is your season!

CHAPTER ONE

THE POWER OF SYNERGIZATION

"Synergization transforms individual efforts
into a force of exponential power.

UNDERSTANDING THE UNDENIABLE
POWER OF SYNERGY

T he word Synergy, in its most basic definition, is the interaction or cooperation of two or more agents, systems, or organizations that produce an effect that is greater than the sum of their individual contributions; now, pay attention to this profound illustration that will help you understand the immense power of synergy in our everyday lives and how it can exponentially increase our collective impact. If, for example, I bring $100, and three more people bring $100 into one basket, how much do we have? That is about $400, right? Now, how about if six more people join the four of us to bring $100 each? How much would we have then? That is about $1,000, isn't it? And if 11 more people were to add to our growing collective, then how much would we have? That would be $2,000, wouldn't it? Can you see how the effect is increasing, and that which could not be done by one person is steadily being achieved by the combined and synergized effort of more people, agents, and elements?

Now, let us push our thinking even further a bit, how about if we decide to buy a house with that money, will it be enough? Of course not! You may not even be able to rent a good place in certain locations with that amount. But here is where the true power of synergy begins to manifest itself in ways that will astound you and revolutionize your understanding of synergizations. What will happen if 200,000 people decide to come out and each of them comes with $2000? How much are we going to have then? That is about $400,000,000, right? Now, add that with the $2000 we initially had, and we are looking at a staggering amount of $400,002,000. Now, do you think we can get a good house with that amount? Of course, we absolutely can! But how was this impossible feat achieved? It was achieved through the undeniable and transformative power of synergy!

Something interesting you should know about synergy is that it does not just work like an addition mentality; it operates on a much more profound and multiplicative level that can exponentially increase our collective impact. Let us go back to our illustration so that you can understand this more deeply. So, at first, 20 people were able to raise $2000, but then what did it attract? It attracted more people who were no longer coming with $100 each but with our total, our initial "whole." In other words, the way Synergy works is that if there's Synergy between two components, it first creates a whole, and that "whole" begins to attract other "wholes" that look like the initial existing whole. This principle is beautifully illustrated in the Bible, specifically in Deuteronomy 32:30 (KJV), which tells us that "one will chase a thousand, and two will put ten thousand to flight" This scripture is letting us know that one will chase a thousand, and two will chase ten thousand, why did it not say two will chase two thousand? It is because synergization goes far beyond the dimension and power of addition into multiplicative and exponential results.

It is like the principle of compound interest because Synergy forces the compounding of the expected result, creating a snowball effect that can lead to unimaginable achievements and breakthroughs in various aspects of our lives. When you understand and apply this principle, you will be opening yourself up to possibilities that were previously beyond your reach, thereby being enabled to accomplish results that were impossible through your individual effort alone.

Let me show you another powerful scripture that explains the importance and effectiveness of synergization in our lives. Ecclesiastes 4:9-12 (KJV) "Two are better than one, because they have a good reward for their labour. For if they fall, the one will lift his fellow: but woe to him that is alone when he falleth; for he hath not another to help him up. Again, if two lie together, then they have heat: but how can one be warm alone? And if one prevails against him, two shall withstand him; and a threefold cord is not quickly broken." This passage beautifully illustrates how synergy not only increases our productivity and rewards but also provides support, strength, and resilience in the face of challenges and adversities.

As we move deeper in this study of understanding the power of synergy, I want you to recognize that this principle extends far beyond mere numerical or financial advantages. Synergy has the potential and power to transform every aspect of your lives, from your personal relationships to your professional endeavors, and even to your spiritual life, especially when you become synergized with the prophet of your life and with the Spirit of God. When you learn to harness the power of synergization, I assure you that the wellspring of collective power, wisdom, strength, strategy, and other glorious resources will begin to gravitate toward you and your destiny with unprecedented momentum and effectiveness.

In the pursuit of destiny, synergization has the power to unlock doors you previously thought were impenetrable because by combining your unique talents, skills, and perspectives with other people, systems, agents, and organizations that God has ordained to be part of your life, you will be able to create a dynamic force that is capable of overcoming obstacles and achieving results that far surpass what any single individual may have ever been able to achieve alone. Has it not dawned on you that there is no man on earth who ever achieved destiny without the powers of synergization? No man can achieve destiny alone, you must synergize with resources, systems, men, and even spirits else you will never be able to achieve all that God designed you to achieve. This is why successful organizations and movements throughout history have always been built on the foundation of effective collaboration and synergy among their members.

Also, in our spiritual lives, synergization plays a very important role, especially in our growth and effectiveness as believers, this is because when we come together in unity and purpose, we are able to create an environment where the Holy Spirit can move powerfully, bringing about transformation not only in our own lives but also in the world around us. This is why the early church, as described in the book of Acts, was able to turn the world upside down despite facing immense opposition and challenges, they truly recognized the power of synergizing with one another and so they became an unstoppable force in their mission of spreading the Gospel and bringing about radical change in society.

Now that we are just begging, before we go very deep, I want you to always remember that this principle is not just a theoretical concept, it is practical wisdom that you must desire to apply in your life every day. Whether it is in your family, your workplace, and especially your spiritual life you must consciously activate the powers of synergization

The undeniable power of synergy goes beyond mere collaboration, it is the key to exponential growth and multiplication of results because when we synergize ourselves with God and others, our capacity increases, our influence grows, and we begin to operate in realms far beyond our natural abilities. Synergy is a divine principle that ensures that our efforts are not wasted, but instead, they yield far greater results than we could ever achieve on our own. Psalm 133:1-3 (KJV), explains it in a beautiful way by saying *"Behold, how good and how pleasant it is for brethren to dwell together in unity! It is like the precious ointment upon the head, that ran down upon the beard, even Aaron's beard: that went down to the skirts of his garments; As the dew of Hermon, and as the dew that descended upon the mountains of Zion: for there the Lord commanded the blessing, even life for evermore."* Do you see it? Anywhere there is synergy, God always commands His blessings to be there. Therefore, if you want to live a life filled with blessings, powers, and divine favor of God, you must embrace Synergization today!

Synergizing In The Creation Of Man

Synergizing With God

When God was about to create man, He said something very weighty that we often overlook, but it holds great significance if we are ever going to understand what God is revealing to us right now. In Genesis 1:26 (KJV), God said, "Let us make man in our image, after our likeness: and let them have dominion over the fish of the sea, and over the fowl of the air, and over the cattle, and over all the earth, and over every creeping thing that creepeth upon the earth." I want you to take note of the words, "Let us."

When you look at the word "let us" it is a revelation of divine synergization at work in our very creation. When He was making the Earth and every other thing in it, we did not hear Him say, "Let us," He kept saying "Let there be light," "Let there be this," and "Let there be that." The Holy Spirit said, "I was wisdom and I stood in His presence when He was creating the Earth," which means the Spirit of God was there, and Jesus, the Word of God, was there, but God was making and creating things by Himself until it got to man, and then He said "let us." In other words, when it came to man, God said let us synergize. He chose to synergize the power of the Trinity – Father, Son, and Holy Spirit to create us.

Do not miss this important point, for it is the key to unlocking your true potential and stepping into the fullness of what God has designed you to be; at the end of the day, the man they came together to make now had authority over the earth. No animal, no species, and not even angels or demons have ever been given authority over the universe, but man was given authority over the earth. Psalm 115:16 (KJV) puts it this way, "The heaven, even the heavens, are the Lord's: but the earth hath he given to the children of men." This is showing us the unique position and authority that mankind holds as a result of the synergized effort of the Godhead in our creation.

A major reason God did this was because He intended that under the governing influence of man, the earth would become the headquarters through which all of His creations would be controlled. In other words, everything, thrones, galaxies, dominions, spirits, and everything that you may not even know about were all intended to be under the governing influence of man. This also means that the synergy of the Godhead ensured that man would not just multiply and replenish the earth, but that man would also have the authority of the Trinity; man would have authority just like God. I need you to take some time and meditate on this because this is meant to bring you light, and it is through the light of knowledge that you will reign in life as well as reach everything God wants for you.

The necessity of all this is that you need to realize that if man operates as a single individual, he will easily be defeated by the world and all the challenges in it, but the synergy of the Father, Son, and the Holy Spirit which created man was supposed to continually radiate through man in such a way that when the universe looks at man, it doesn't just see man as one creature which is completely insignificant, unimportant, and irrelevant; rather, when the universe looks at us, it should see the totality of divinity radiating in glory through us.

Here is where we are going to, in order for you to be the

master of life on Earth and in the whole universe, just as the book of Colossians tells us that Jesus will rule over everything, thrones, dominions, universe etc., God has ordained that certain components must come together. Yes, you as an individual may be good, but you need the synergization of other necessary agents, systems, organizations, and even spirits so that your life will begin to produce a kind of result that far supersedes your individual capacity and capability as a person.

Let me show you something that many believers are missing, and this revelation has the power to transform your understanding of yourself and your potential in Christ completely. Take the human body for example; you see, the entire human body is controlled by certain systems, we have the digestive system, the nervous system, the respiratory system, the skeletal system, and even more, they are all properly synergized so that we can function and live healthy as human beings. When you think about the structural system for example, which includes your skeletal structure, if one disk is removed from a person's spinal cord, do you realize that that person may never be the same again? And yes, medical doctors may be able to surgically adjust and help with some treatments, but there is a probability that such a person may forever live by drugs all the days of their lives. This is because a major component that is supposed to be synergized with other parts of that person's body has been lost. How about when someone dies? You will see their bones scattered everywhere. What this means is that we human beings are a product of many synergized parts working together; there are over 300 bones in the human body, yet when just one is removed, that person becomes troubled for life.

Many people are supposed to be synergized with several systems and components in life, but because they are not, they are not yet experiencing the stability, progress, and achievement that is necessary for their lives. If you want to truly see the power you have and how strong you were created to be, then you must be set to see all components rightly work together. But the number one person you must learn to synergize with is God! If you do not know how to synergize with God, then there are levels and dimensions of glory and destiny that you will never step into. If you read 1 Corinthians 3:9 you will see that it reveals the divine intention for us to work in synergy with God Himself, co-laboring with the Creator of the universe to bring about His purposes on earth; it is through this powerful alignment that God's will and allow His power to work through you as you tap into Him as your source of divine strength and wisdom that far exceeds our human limitations.

Also, in Philippians 2:13 (KJV), the bible says, "For it is God which worketh in you both to will and to do of his good pleasure." The verse reveals that there is an internal synergy between our will and God's will, our actions and God's power working through us. When you learn to synergize with God in this way, you become a vessel through which His divine power can flow towards accomplishing great things.

Synergization in The Body

Synergy with God is just the beginning of what He has in store for us, the Lord also intends that as a church we become synergized with ourselves, I know I have talked about synergizing with others before but right now I am placing emphasis on us as a body of Christ synergizing with each other, creating a network of divine connections that can unleash unprecedented levels of power and effectiveness in our lives. In 1 Corinthians 12:12-27, the Apostle Paul uses the analogy of the human body to describe how we as different members of the church are meant to work together in synergy with each part fulfilling its unique function but all working together for the common good and the advancement of God's kingdom.

Also, when it comes to spiritual gifts and callings, synergy plays an important role in the effectiveness of the body of Christ.

Romans 12:4-5 (KJV) tells us, "For as we have many members in one body, and all members have not the same office: So, we, being many, are one body in Christ, and every one members one of another." This is a revelation of the necessity of different gifts and callings working together in synergy for the overall effectiveness of the church. This means that when we recognize our interdependence and learn to operate in harmony with one another, we are able to create an environment where the power of God can flow freely, bringing about transformation and breakthrough in ways that would be impossible if we were operating in isolation.

I want you to also think about the synergy between a husband and wife in marriage, Genesis 2:24 (KJV) says "Therefore shall a man leave his father and his mother and shall cleave unto his wife: and they shall be one flesh." This is not about physical union; it is about two people coming together in a synergization that creates something greater than each of them can produce alone. When a husband and wife learn to synergize their strengths, compensate for each other's weaknesses, and unite in purpose and vision, they become a powerful force for good in their family, their community, and even in the world at large.

Remember, you were created through divine synergization, and you were created for synergization. When you begin to operate in this truth, you will find strength you never knew you had, and you will discover that those challenges which look unbeatable now are nothing but mountains you can crush anytime you like. So, I challenge you today, seek out the synergizations that God has ordained for your life. Look for ways to align your will with God's will, find opportunities to combine your strengths with the strengths of others, and desire mentors and partners who can complement your weaknesses and amplify your strengths. And no matter what happens, never forget that you are the product of divine synergy, created to operate in synergy, and destined to achieve greatness through synergization.

CHAPTER TWO

THE MYSTERIES AND ADVENTURES OF LIFE

Challenges are not barriers, they are the adventures that destiny uses to draw out the powers inside of you.

WHY DO WE EXPERIENCE BAD THINGS IN LIFE

Repeatedly, I keep hearing people say, "Why does God allow bad things to happen to us, even though we are His children? Why do good people experience bad things? Why can't life be simple, smooth, and always pleasing, without trouble or crisis?" Well, I want you to know that if life were always easy, it would become very, very boring, and almost meaningless. What makes life truly adventurous and worth living are the victories and testimonies we achieve. When everything goes smoothly without challenges, life becomes dull and soon begins to feel empty. You soon feel like it is a waste of time because there are no obstacles to overcome, no moments of triumph to celebrate.

When we took our kids to learn coding, at first, they were excited but soon, they began to complain. When I inquired, they said,

"Dad, this is too simple, we have moved past this level." Do you see what I am getting at? When things become too easy, we start to feel like they are not worth our time. Life is meant to be an adventure, a journey where we keep fighting, battling, and conquering. Since we are created to be synergized with the Trinity within us, God allows that power within us to draw challenges from around us, so the greatness inside can find full expression and bring us fulfillment.

Let me explain, If God has placed power within you, how will that power manifest if there are no battles to conquer? If God has given you the ability to heal, how will that ability find expression if there are no sick people? There was a man who once said to his children, "If God wanted humans to fly, He would have given them wings," yet he kept preaching that God is supernatural, powerful, and able to do the impossible. Ironically, it was those same children who later invented the airplane. Yes, there were prototypes before, but it was these children who took it a step further and perfected flight.

I want you to understand that often, the adventures and challenges that God has ordained to push you into your destiny are all around you, and you have labeled them as "troubles." Another way to put it is that "adventures" and "troubles" are the very things God has ordained to propel you into your place of destiny and glorious manifestation. When the destiny God has placed within you starts seeking expression and fulfillment, it begins to call for itself from outside of you. This calling is what we often label as "trouble." So, the next time you face difficulties, remember that it is not just trouble, it is the destiny within you calling for fulfillment outside of you.

Count it all Joy

In James 1:2-4 (KJV) the bible says, "My brethren, count it all joy when you fall into divers temptations; Knowing this, that the trying of your faith worketh patience. But let patience have her perfect work, that you may be perfect and entire, wanting nothing." Here, James is telling us that our trials and our troubles are working something in us, and they are producing patience, maturity, and completeness in us so that we can be ready for our great destiny! Think about the life of Joseph in the Bible, he was a young man with dreams of greatness, but His journey was far from smooth, in fact, he faced betrayal from his brothers, he was thrown in a pit, sold into slavery, and also suffered false accusations alongside and imprisonment. Yet, each of these "troubles" was a steppingstone towards his ultimate destiny. All his troubles were just destiny from the outside calling to the destiny on His inside His time as a slave in Potiphar's house taught him management skills; His years in prison honed his ability to interpret dreams even more; all these experiences prepared him for his role as second-in-command of Egypt, where he saved countless lives during a severe famine. Can you see it? What initially looked like trouble was destiny on the outside calling to destiny on His inside.

Or think about David, the shepherd boy who became king, His battles with lions and bears while tending sheep were all preparing him for his encounter with Goliath. His years of running from Saul taught him leadership and strategy, all of which were skills he needed as king. Even his great sin and subsequent repentance deepened his relationship with God, leading to many of the Psalms we cherish today. Or do you want to talk about Paul who was formerly Saul? He was a persecutor of the church but his dramatic conversion on the road to Damascus was just the beginning because he later faced beatings, shipwrecks, imprisonments, and even more. Yet each of these trials were what shaped him into being one of the greatest apostles to have ever lived and even authored more books in the New Testament. Truly, his troubles became the very tools God used to fulfill his destiny.

Romans 8:28 (KJV) gives us a powerful assurance by saying, "And we know that all things work together for good to them that love

God, to them who are the called according to his purpose." This verse does not say only good things happen to those who love God, instead, it promises us that ALL things, including what we see as troubles are working together for our good and for our destiny. Now, I am not saying you should go looking for trouble or that you should enjoy suffering. Not at all! But I am saying that when troubles come, and they will come you should look at them through a different lens and you should see them not as mere obstacles or punishments, but as potential launch pads for your destiny because as long as you are synergized with God, no weapon formed against you can truly destroy you, they will only serve to set you for destiny.

Have you ever thought about how a diamond, one of the most precious and beautiful gems in the world is formed? They are formed under enormous pressure and heat deep within the earth. Without that pressure, that "trouble," the diamond would never come to be. In the same way, the pressures, and troubles you are facing are meant to create something beautiful and valuable in you as long as you are synergized with God.

Many times, in life we are always praying for God to remove our troubles and to make our paths smooth, but you need to realize that in His wisdom, God knows that these very troubles are essential for your growth, your strengthening, your preparation for the destiny He has for you. This is a perspective of hope it may not make your troubles go away but it will give you the strength to go through them like a student writing an exam and pass out with flying colors. That challenge may be tough, but I want you to draw hope in the midst of that difficulty, knowing that it will be used by God for your good and His glory.

I declare in the name of Jesus that those troubles are not the end of your story, they are just the beginning of a new chapter, a chapter where you grow stronger, wiser, and more resilient. A chapter where you become more of who God created you to be. And a chapter that prepares you for the great things God has in store for you.

How God Uses Your Troubles To Forge You When
You Are Properly Synergized With Him

God is saying to you today "I am going to use all your troubles to synergize your purpose to synergize your destiny and to produce a living and miraculous wonder out of your life" but How does God do It?

Resilience:

He allows your troubles to build something called "resilience" because he knows you will need it if you are going to win the battles waiting for you at the top. Resilience is not just about bouncing back; it is about bouncing forward and the ability to not only recover from your setbacks and challenges but to grow through them. I want you to imagine resilience as a spiritual and emotional muscle, then realize that just as physical muscles grow stronger through resistance training, our resilience grows stronger through the resistance of life's challenges. One notable example of resilience in the bible is Job who lost everything, his wealth, his children, his health, and yet he remained faithful to God. His story teaches us that resilience doesn't just mean you need to avoid pain or pretend everything is fine. It's about maintaining faith and integrity even when life is at its hardest. Job 23:10 (KJV) "But he knoweth the way that I take: when he hath tried me, I shall come forth as gold." We talked about Paul earlier, and in 2 Corinthians 4:8-9 (KJV), "We are troubled on every side, yet not distressed; we are perplexed, but not in despair; Persecuted, but not forsaken; cast down, but not destroyed." This is resilience in action, facing troubles without being overwhelmed, experiencing confusion without losing hope, enduring persecution without feeling abandoned, and being knocked down but not knocked out.

Unlocking and Clarifying Purpose:

God uses your trials to unlock and clarify your purpose to you, there are many people who would never truly discover what they are here to do on earth without their troubles. Sometimes you may think as man that you are here to do many things, but then you may notice that there is a particular challenge that keeps hitting you and hitting you repeatedly. But you also keep hitting back again and again, when this continually happens, after a while, you will develop mastery in dealing with this particular situation, and by the time you look at your life, you will discover you are also not where you used to be rather you have moved, you have grown, you are wiser, better and even strong in every sense. This is when God will now say, it is time to rescue others, it is time to teach others how to conquer this also. Think about Esther, whose purpose was clarified through the threat to her people, it was in the face of this trouble that Mordecai reminded her, "Who knoweth whether thou art come to the kingdom for such a time as this?" (Esther 4:14, KJV). Her trial revealed and clarified her purpose - to save her people.

Your Pain Points to Your Call:

Some of us as human beings will only find Purpose when life troubles us a lot because most times the things that trouble you are the troubles you are born to solve, most times the things that irritate you are the problems you are called to solve, so you may think that life is defeating you whereas God has called you to turn losers into Champions you may not know how it's going to happen but just trust God. God allows trouble to reveal your calling. In the Bible, we see this principle at work in the life of Nehemiah. His distress over the state of Jerusalem's walls was the revealer of his call to rebuild them. Nehemiah 1:4 (KJV) tells us "And it came to pass, when I heard these words, that I sat down and wept, and mourned certain days, and fasted, and prayed before the God of heaven." When you are properly synergized with God, He allows you to experience and even witness pain not because He wants you to be defeated, but to direct you and point you to your purpose and calling through those pains.

Troubles Unlock Creativity Within You:

In this realm of creativity, you begin to operate in a level of innovation and wisdom that is supernatural, through your troubles and problems, wisdom can come upon you. I know you may be embarrassed by your contradictions today, but I want you to know that they are working in you an eternal weight of glory. I know there may be several prophecies in your life and you are probably complaining, "God said I will build houses for people and become a billionaire, yet I am still struggling to survive" "The Lord Prophesied that I will lay hands on the sick and they will be healed, yet I am still struggling with my health" well I want you to know that God is not done with you yet, he did not lie to you, you are only going through the training phase of that great destiny, and through your challenges, God is trying to synergize and synchronize you with His purpose and ultimate assignment for your life. Even as you read this, I see God unlocking creativity within you, creativity that will grant you the ability to look at complex situations and turn them into great opportunities in Jesus' name. In Exodus 31:3 (KJV), we read about Bezalel, who was filled "with the spirit of God, in wisdom, and in understanding, and in knowledge, and in all manner of workmanship." This divine creativity allowed him to craft the delicate elements of the Tabernacle. So also, when you face troubles and are properly synergized with God, He will be able to fill you with His wisdom, understanding, and knowledge to creatively deal with those situations.

Troubles Come to Unlock Speed:

The troubles of life are meant to unlock speed within you, in this life all of us do not move at the same levels of speed. Some people make progress with the speed of a chameleon while others make progress with the speed of a Cheetah, but when you go through trials, you begin to develop a level of strength and abilities that someone who has been enjoying a soft life will never have, it may look like they are enjoying, but in truth their progress will be slow, because they do not have the fires of refinement (troubles) to push them beyond their limits, beyond their comfort zones and beyond their current state of complacency. When troubles come, they put pressure on you so that you can master start things and gain speed, have you ever been burnt by fire, perhaps a stove? Did you delightfully leave your hand in the fire? I am sure you took it off in a hurry, that is my point so many would have remained completely useless in life except for the troubles that pushed them into destiny by force. There are several people who because of their challenges vowed to themselves that they will never remain in that low situation and that they must get out of this situation quickly enough fast enough.

Synergization with the Lord makes our troubles create a holy dissatisfaction in our hearts with the status quo, a divine urgency that propels us forward at a speed we never thought possible. It is as if our troubles light a fire under us, pushing us to grow, learn, and achieve at an accelerated rate.

Don't Allow Your Synergy Be Corrupted

Let us now go back again to Genesis 1, where God said let us make man in our image, what this means is that man was inside God, and the man inside God kept calling the man outside God, but as at this time God was in a Chaotic environment, empty mass, empty space and when God showed up, He also wanted to see man in full manifestation, this is why when you read Genesis 1 you will see God preparing things, calling light, calling fish, creating animal and every other thing by calling them to be, he was taking care of the chaotic situation so that he can bring out the man that was inside him.

One thing you should realize here is that Synergy can be corrupted, and God knew this, this is why he never allowed the Darkness and the light to stay together. After God called the light by saying let there be light, he was pleased with the light and because he didn't want any form of corruption, he decided to separate the light from the darkness, Genesis 1:4 tells us "And God saw the light, that it was good: and God divided the light from the darkness." Many people today have become corrupted, they stayed with bad friends, corrupted themselves on the bed of fornication, corrupted themselves with amoral behaviors and so many other forms of corruption. But today, it is time for you to make amends, it is time to look at your life and just like God did, it is time to separate the darkness from the Light of your life.

This is not just about corruption and sin only, every part of your life that looks dark right now, maybe health challenge, maybe demonic battles, all these are also corruptions because they are part of the works of darkness, so darkness is not just you committing sin alone, it's also every work of the devil trying to destroy your destiny and you can take it away from your life, you can command it to go away, YES! You can command every works of darkness to be removed from your territory, your life, and your destiny.

When God separated the light from the darkness it was also a prophetic declaration of God saying "hey darkness, I will put my light in man and man will cooperate with me and from that day, man will make sure that you are inconsequential" This is why we can boldly see in John 1:4 that the bible says "In him was life; and the life was the light of men." Can you see that Christ will be the light of men? Verse 5 then tells us that this light which is now in men will shine in darkness and darkness will not be able to comprehend, defeat, understand, subdue, or overcome it.

This revelation of maintaining the purity of your synergization with God is important for your spiritual well-being and attainment of destiny. Just as God separated light from darkness in creation, we are called to be vigilant in separating the light of God's presence in our lives from the darkness of sin and worldly influences. Apostle Paul also taught this in 2 Corinthians

6:14 (KJV), saying, "Be you not unequally yoked together with unbelievers: for what fellowship hath righteousness with unrighteousness? and what communion hath light with darkness?" This shows the importance of maintaining the purity of your spiritual synergy. You cannot expect to walk in close fellowship with God while simultaneously embracing the ways of the world, that's impossible, true synergization with the Lord does not walk like that.

1 John 1:5-7 (KJV) puts it this way "This then is the message which we have heard of him, and declare unto you, that God is light, and in him is no darkness at all. If we say that we have fellowship with him, and walk in darkness, we lie, and do not the truth: But if we walk in the light, as he is in the light, we have fellowship one with another, and the blood of Jesus Christ his Son cleanseth us from all sin."

Don't forget this very important point; and because it's very important I will emphasize it again, "the corruption of your synergy with God doesn't always come in obvious forms, sometimes, it's the subtle influences" a little compromise here, a white lie there, a moment of gossiping, all these are the things that can begin to erode your relationship with God because these small corruptions can accumulate over time, gradually dimming the light of God in your life.

That's why the bible tells us in the book of Revelation that a day is coming when Jesus will be the light and man will no longer need any other light because the light of God will fill the earth, I am not talking about Jesus as "God", I am talking about Jesus "the man" with his pierced hands and wounded feet shall rule the earth and there will be no more night. Night here is also symbolic of the mockery of the enemy, the sickness that the enemy brings, no more demonic oppression, no more demonic possession, no more death, and more pain, etc. This is synergy indeed! God synergizing with man and we shall all reign forever. Read it for yourself Revelation 21:23-25 (KJV) "And the city had no need of the sun, neither of the moon, to shine in it: for the glory of God did lighten it, and the Lamb is the light thereof. And the nations of them which are saved shall walk in the light of it: and the kings of the earth do bring their glory and honor into it. And the gates of it shall not be shut at all by day: for there shall be no night there." This prophetic vision shows us the goal of our synergization with God, a perfect, uncorrupted communion where His light dispels all darkness.

So you may be in a season where so many troubles may be tagging along with your life as you walk on the path of destiny, well I am saying don't worry, that challenge cannot be there forever, they only came with to you because of the glory within you attracting them, but remember, these troubles are not meant to corrupt your synergization with God, instead, they are opportunities to strengthen your relationship with Him and to make you rely more fully on His strength and wisdom.

Here are some guidelines to help you maintain the purity of your synergization and dispel darkness from your life.

- Daily prayer and Bible study to stay connected to the source of light.

- Regular self-examination and repentance to address any areas of darkness creeping into our lives.

- Surrounding ourselves with godly influences and accountability partners who can help us stay on track.

- Actively resisting temptation and fleeing from sin, as Paul instructed Timothy to "Flee also youthful lusts: but follow righteousness, faith, charity, peace, with them that call on the Lord out of a pure heart." (2 Timothy 2:22, KJV)

- Continuously filling our minds with things that are pure and godly, as instructed in Philippians 4:8 (KJV): "Finally, brethren, whatsoever things are true, whatsoever things are honest, whatsoever things are just, whatsoever things are pure, whatsoever things are lovely, whatsoever things are of good report; if there be any virtue, and if there be any praise, think on these things."

Remember, the goal is not perfection, but progress, you will stumble at times, but what matters is that you get back up, reorient yourself toward God's light, and continue moving forward. I beseech you by the mercies of God, never allow your synergy with God to be corrupted, guard it zealously, nurture it daily, and watch as it transforms not only your life but the lives of those around you. For in maintaining this pure connection with God, you become a beacon of His light in a world desperately in need of illumination.

CHAPTER THREE

THE PATH OF PREPARATION FOR DESTINY

"Before greatness can manifest, the environment must be right"

PREPARE YOUR ENVIRONMENT

Something else you should also note in Genesis 1 is that before bringing forth man the Lord took time to prepare the environment. This is where many people are failing in life; they keep destroying their lives, their ambitions, and the intentions of God for them because they have failed to prepare their environment! They are so much in a hurry to fulfill their destiny that they have failed to prepare their environment for it, and I need you to know that no matter how hard you labor to bring out your destiny if you are in the wrong environment, you will destroy that destiny by yourself. Think about a flower trying to survive in an environment covered by weeds; that is exactly what you are doing if you do not first prepare your environment like God did before finally saying, "Let us make man." He knew that without the right environment, man would not thrive.

Man originated from the inside of God; he was in God. That is why God could say, "Let us make man." Do you think it's normal that your inside is proclaiming that you are great? Deep within your spirit, you already know that you are great, so take time to prepare your environment, and you will see that greatness finding expression. You can never have a great and strong desire to be a billionaire, for example, if there is no billionaire inside you. So, each time you have a great desire for a great destiny, just know that it is because greatness already lives within you, and it is trying to come out. So many others also fail because they always allow the voice of greatness within them to be silenced by the voice of challenges and other contradicting voices outside them. You must make up your mind today that no matter what you do, you will never allow that voice on your inside to die. The Bible says in Colossians 1:27 (KJV), "*To whom God would make known what is the riches of the glory of this mystery among the Gentiles*; which is Christ in you, the hope of glory." Do you hear the words "Christ in you" The word of God is talking about glory within you. But that glory is trapped on the inside of you, and a glory locked within you is not yet true glory, that glory must begin to radiate until men can see your good works and glorify your Father which is in heaven.

Child of God, no matter what you do in life, do not try to occupy a stage you are not properly prepared for, because the wind outside will destroy that which you are about to birth. During the period of creation, there was no day when God created just a single element, but when it came to man, only he was made on the sixth day. Do you know why? Because God first took His time to prepare the earth for man; simply put "the earth was made for man and not man for the Earth." This should tell you how valuable you are in God's eyes. Take a look at the parable of the sower in Matthew 13:3-9 (KJV): "*And he spake many things unto them in parables, saying, Behold, a sower went forth to sow; And when he sowed, some seeds fell by the wayside, and the fowls came and devoured them up: Some fell upon stony places, where they had not much earth: and forthwith they sprung up, because they had no deepness of earth: And when the sun was up, they were scorched; and because they had no root, they withered away. And some fell among thorns; and the thorns sprung up, and choked them: But other fell into good ground, and brought forth fruit, some an hundredfold, some sixtyfold, some thirtyfold. Who hath ears to hear, let him hear."*

This parable reveals to us again the importance of preparing your environment, the seed, which represents your destiny, your God-given potential, can only truly thrive when it falls on good ground, a well-prepared environment. Just as a farmer doesn't simply throw seeds anywhere and expect a bountiful harvest, you cannot expect your destiny to flourish in an unprepared environment.

So, what does it mean to prepare your environment? It means cultivating and synergizing yourself with the right mindset, surrounding yourself with the right people, acquiring the necessary knowledge and skills, and most importantly, making sure your heart is in line with God's purpose for your life. This is how you remove the 'weeds' of negative influences, the 'stones' of past hurts and unforgiveness, and the 'thorns' of worldly distractions that wants to choke your spiritual growth. How do you think it would have been if God created Adam and then started thinking about where to put him? That would be absurd, right? Of course it will be, so instead of doing that he He prepared the Garden of Eden first, a perfect environment for man to thrive and fulfill his purpose. In the same way, God is calling you to prepare your 'garden' - your mind, your heart, your relationships, your skills so that when He plants the seed of your destiny, it will find fertile soil to grow and bear fruit.

Before You Were Formed

In Jeremiah 1:5 (KJV), the word of God tells us "Before I formed thee in the belly I knew thee; and before thou camest forth out of the womb I sanctified thee, and I ordained thee a prophet unto the nations." This is a strong reminder that God has a plan for each of us, a destiny He prepared before we were even born, and just as He prepared us for our destiny, we must prepare our environment to receive and nurture that destiny. Preparing your environment also means being patient, you do not have to rush into things you are not ready for. God took six days to create the world, not because He could not do it in an instant, but to teach us the importance of process and preparation. Each day of creation was a step towards the goal, "the creation of man." In the same way, each step you take in preparing your environment is a step towards the manifestation of your God-given destiny. Therefore, my friend, take a moment to look at your life. Are you in a hurry to achieve your dreams without proper preparation? Are you trying to force your destiny in an environment that is not ready to sustain it? Remember, a seed planted in unprepared soil may sprout quickly, but it will wither just as fast when the heat comes. But a seed planted in well-prepared soil will grow strong roots, withstand the storms, and produce a bountiful harvest.

Start today and begin to weed out negative influences from your life! Start cultivating good habits that are in line with your goals; surround yourself with people who inspire you and can challenge you to grow; invest in knowledge and skills that will be necessary for your destiny; and most importantly position your life in line with God's purpose for your life.

You are God's masterpiece and created for greatness, but even masterpieces need the right environment to shine. So, prepare your environment and watch as God brings forth the man/woman of destiny that He has ordained you to be.

The Mystery Of The Dust

When God was ready to call forth His man, the same man that was inside Him, where did he come from? The man came from dust. The very same man, which was inside God, which God wanted to bring to manifestation, came out from dust, can you imagine that? I want you to know that those things that God told you about concerning your life may not always look like what you want to see when you get to see it, because it might look like dirt, it might look like dust, it might look ugly, it may look like a stone which the builders reject, and it may look like nothing good can come out of it. But this is where the power of synergization steps in, because as you begin to release God's power within you, partnering with God and following His instructions, you will suddenly realize that your destiny which looks like dust, soon begins to look amazing.

Yes, on the inside you are a billionaire, but on the outside, you may not even be able to pay your rent and you may not be able to pay your other fees, but as you begin to mold it just like the Lord, and as you pick that dust, you will soon realize that through the power of synergizing with God, you can turn that dust into gold, into beauty, and into glory. I don't care what you may be going through, I don't care if you look like dust now, but I want you to know that those thoughts of greatness and desires within you are responding to something that you can be on the outside, and as you begin to synergize with the Lord, you will soon realize that the health problem is gone, the financial challenge is gone, and all other kinds of challenges you may be going through are gone.

Look at the story of David in 1 Samuel 16:11-13 (KJV) *"And Samuel said unto Jesse, Are here all thy children? And he said, There remaineth yet the youngest, and, behold, he keepeth the sheep. And Samuel said unto Jesse, Send and fetch him: for we will not sit down till he come hither. And he sent, and brought him in. Now he was ruddy, and withal of a beautiful countenance, and goodly to look to. And the Lord said, Arise, anoint him: for this is he. Then Samuel took the horn of oil, and anointed him in the midst of his brethren: and the Spirit of the Lord came upon David from that day forward. So Samuel rose up, and went to Ramah."* David was the least and on the outside and he looked like dust so nobody ever imagined he would be the candidate that God was going to anoint for kingship. He was the youngest, a mere shepherd boy, and even overlooked even by his own father. In the eyes of the world, he was truly 'dust' but God saw beyond the dust,

He saw a king, a man after His own heart and this is the mystery of the dust "that which seems insignificant in the eyes of the world can become great in the hands of God."

I know life may be tough now, but the mystery of dust is that when your heart as the heart of man begins to cooperate with the heart of the Father, Son, and Spirit, then synergization can happen; and when that happens, you will realize that God created you to be a solution to the world, an agent of change, an agent of glory, an agent of power. When men look at you, you will know it is not just by your strength; rather, it is the product of synergizing and becoming one with the Spirit of God.

It is really a powerful thing when your heart synergizes with God, this is when, although you are a single person, you will begin to function like an entire army. Look at David, again, how do you think he conquered Goliath? It was through synergization! The entire army could not kill Goliath, but when David came, because he was synergized with God, it did not matter if he were a small boy or if in the eyes of the people and Goliath, he looked like dust. At the end of the day, he killed that giant which had been terrorizing the army for many days with just a sling. When you get to this level, people will be shocked at the results that your life will produce. They will start asking questions, saying, "How are you able to do it?" And all you will say is, "It is because I have synergized with the Lord."

Problems are Looking for solutions

It has been confirmed that problems normally gravitate towards not just a solution, but they gravitate towards the best solutions, so each time you see problems, I want you to know that God is trying to show you something. You may see it as problems, trials, and challenges, but those are your doorways to destiny. Why does it "look like" money is running away from you? It is because you have the power and ability to catch it, multiply it, and distribute it. So, if it comes, you may become complacent with just a little change and settle for less, when God has destined you for wealth and abundance. Therefore, by running away from you, it is trying to show you that you can go after it, subdue it, multiply it, and through it become a solution to the world by being a financial helper to many people.

God does not want you to be in a hurry in destiny, He took His time to put over 300 bones in man; after putting over 200, He kept adding until it was complete. If you are in a hurry concerning destiny, you will never be able to synergize with God's ideology well, and so you will not be able to produce His kind of result. This was what happened to Joseph in Genesis 37-50. Over and over again Joseph's dreams of greatness seemed to turn to dust when he was placed in the pit, sold into slavery, and then thrown into prison, but God was working even in those dusty, dark places. Each setback was a setup for Joseph's ultimate destiny and what looked like dust to others was the raw material God was using to shape a leader who would save nations. Oh, Child of God, do not despise the dust in your life, do not be discouraged by the seemingly insignificant or difficult circumstances you find yourself in. They are the raw materials through which the Lord is perfecting for destiny and just as a sculptor does not see a block of marble as a hindrance but as the medium for his masterpiece, God sees the 'dust' of your life as the perfect material for crafting your destiny.

Remember, that gold is refined by fire, and pearls are created through irritation, in the same way, your challenges, your struggles, your 'dust' moments are the very things God is using to form something precious and valuable in you. Your financial struggles. They are teaching you stewardship and faith, Your health challenges. They are developing in you compassion and resilience, Your relational difficulties. They are shaping your character and teaching you love and forgiveness. Duts may look dead and useless, but in the hands of our God, that same dust can become life, become beauty, and become destiny. So, I encourage you today to embrace your 'dust', synergize with God in transformation, synergize with His Spirit, and align your heart with His purpose, and you will see that dues turned into a wonder in the mighty name of Jesus.

In essence, you are not defined by how you look now, by your current circumstances, or by what others see; NO! You are defined by what God sees in you, by the potential He has placed within you, so hold on to those dreams and those visions of greatness because they are not mere fantasies; they are the echoes of your true identity, glimpses of your God-ordained destiny and in your synergization with God, you will be able to allow His power to work in and through you, you will see that dust begin to take shape, to come alive, to shine with divine purpose.

God Wants Your Heart To Cooperate With Him

Have you not noticed that many of the components of a man's body are multiple? He has two eyes, two hands, two legs, two kidneys, two ears, but how about the heart? Man has just one heart! Do you know why? Because as you walk through the path of preparation God wants you to focus that heart and synergize it with Him! God does not want your heart divided, and the moment you can truly synergize that heart with Him, then you are set for a breakthrough and a glorious destiny! If Satan attacks your health, that attack is an invitation to tell you that you can synergize with God and become a healer. You are tasting of what others are suffering because God is training you to be their healer. How about if it's a financial challenge? You are being prepared to feel what people are going through so that you will have compassion towards them, then you can effectively synergize with God and then become their helper. The point is that you must give your heart to God and synergize with Him.

Now, if for example, money comes to you a little and stays with you, then it is proof that money thinks you are a loser and you cannot handle it in big measures, so it will stay. But if it leaves, then it's proof that you can synergize your heart with God and begin to experience financial abundance in a glorious measure because you have the ability to catch it and tame it.

The way it works for many people is that when they begin to face financial challenges and health challenges, and they go to God, God will say, "Okay, let me work with you. Look at this financial principle, look at this business principle, check your kingdom giving, check your offerings in church." What is He doing? Because you are cooperating with Him, He is guiding you on how to attain "true riches," not just temporary cash in your hands. In health challenges, it is the same thing. God will begin to train you, take you higher in health issues, and give you some wisdom and even spiritual principles that will help you handle the situations. I want you to know that God wants to take you up, but today God is saying, "My challenge is not taking you up, my challenge is keeping you up, because it's slippery up there, it's windy up there, it's more challenging up there, but guess what? It's better up there."

When I talk about "UP," I am talking about a very deep walk with God and higher places in destiny, It's a stage where you trust Him and you rely on Him because you now know that no man will ever prevail by strength, no man will ever make it by strength, and that it's only by synergization with the Lord that you will ever become a valuable person on earth.

What are some of the strategies that God will teach you here?

Trust:

The Lord will teach you how to trust in Him, this isn't just a superficial trust, but a deep, and unshakable confidence in His plans and timing for your life. Proverbs 3:5-6 (KJV) tells us, "Trust in the Lord with all thine heart; and lean not unto thine own understanding. In all thy ways acknowledge him, and he shall direct thy paths." When you truly achieve synergization with the

Lord in your heart, you will find yourself trusting Him even when circumstances seem dire and you will learn to see challenges not as obstacles, but as opportunities for God to showcase His power in your life.

Wisdom:

God will begin to teach you different kinds of wisdom that are far beyond natural wisdom, I am not just talking about being smart because you went to school. We are talking about divine wisdom, the kind that Solomon had when he asked God for an understanding heart to judge the people. As James 1:5 (KJV) tells us, "If any of you lack wisdom, let him ask of God, that giveth to all men liberally, and upbraideth not; and it shall be given him." synergization helps you tap into a wellspring of wisdom that'll have people wondering how you got so wise.

Strategy:

Strategy means that God will guide you step-by-step on how to fulfill your destiny. God is not just going to dump success in your laps. Nah, He is going teach you how to strategize, how to plan, how to execute. He will show you the chess moves of life and make you a winner in everything you place your hands to do. Do you remember how God gave Joshua the strategy to conquer Jericho? That is the kind of strategic thinking you will develop when you begin to value and prioritize synergization with God.

It will Not Always Make Sense

Now, let me tell you something, when your heart truly synergizes with God, you will start seeing miracles in your life that will blow your mind, you will be walking in levels of prosperity that are beyond your individual capacity, and this Is not just about money alone, I'm talking about prosperity in every area of your life that will make people begin to wonder what your secret is. But here is the thing, this synergization with the Lord may not always be easy. Sometimes, God's will ask you to do things that do not make sense to your natural mind. He might tell you to give when you feel you do not have enough, He might tell you to rest when you feel you should be working. He might tell you to speak when you feel like being quiet, or to be quiet when you feel like speaking. However, let me tell you, when you obey those promptings, that is when you will see the real power of synergizing with God.

Remember the story of Peter in Luke 5:4-6 (KJV)? *"Now when he had left speaking, he said unto Simon, Launch out into the deep, and let down your nets for a draught. And Simon answering said unto him, Master, we have toiled all the night, and have taken nothing: nevertheless at thy word I will let down the net. And when they had this done, they inclosed a great multitude of fishes: and their net brake."* Peter had to synergize his heart with Jesus' instruction, even when it didn't make sense to his professional fisherman's mind. And the result? A catch so big it nearly broke their nets! That is what happens when you synergize your heart with God. You start operating on a different frequency, you start seeing opportunities where others see obstacles, you start turning setbacks into setups for comebacks and You start walking in a level of authority that makes the enemy tremble.

When you start living like this, when you achieve synergization, you become unstoppable. Why? Because it is not just you anymore. It is you and God moving as one and operating in perfect harmony. That is when you will start seeing those billionaire dreams become reality. That is when you will start seeing your health restored in ways that baffle the doctors. That is when you will start seeing doors open that you did not even know existed.

It all starts with your heart, just one heart fully surrendered and fully synergized with the heart of God. That is all it takes to change your world! What are you waiting for?

CHAPTER FOUR

WALKING WITH GOD ON THE HIGH PLACES

"The deeper your walk with God, the more intense the battles, but every gate that stands against you must lift its head when God is on your side."

A DEEPER LEVEL

When you have successfully walked through the path of preparation as the spirit of God has revealed in Chapter Three, you then begin to step into the stage of deeper levels of walking with God. This is the stage where you will begin to encounter several spirits that the Lord will dispatch to guide you through life. I am talking about spirits like the four-faced Spirit that is looking in one direction but sees in every direction. Now, that might sound deep to your natural mind but let me break it down for you.

At this stage, you will be able to look with the face of man, which means you are always looking up to God. You are not depending on your own understanding, but you are constantly seeking God's face, His wisdom, His direction because you are living the reality of Proverbs 3:5-6. This is the foundation of walking with God on the high places.

But it does not stop there, you will also look with the face of a sheep. Now, what does that mean? It means you are maintaining a spirit of humility and submission, you are not trying to be the shepherd, but you are willing to follow where God leads. Remember what Jesus said in John 10:27 (KJV)? "My sheep hear my voice, and I know them, and they follow me." That is the attitude you need to have.

The next is that You will also be able to look with the face of a lion. Why? Because anyone that wants to attack you or take you down, you must be able to defend yourself and defend the visions and destiny which the Lord has committed into your hands. You cannot be weak in this walk, my friend. You need to be bold and courageous, ready to stand firm in your faith and your calling.

And then, you must also look with the face of an eagle, this is important because it means your vision must not be deterred by your warfare. An eagle soars above the storms, and that is exactly what you need to do. No matter what challenges come your way, you must be able to maintain that heavenly perspective, I am talking about that God-given vision for your life.

Now, let us talk about the ox, the ox represents the sacrifice that is always needed for the destiny you are called to fulfill. But listen carefully because this is where many people get it wrong. Your sacrifice is meant to sharpen your vision, not to kill your vision. Too many people think that walking with God on the high places means you must sacrifice everything and live a miserable life. That is not it at all! Your sacrifices should be refining you, making you stronger, more focused, and more determined to fulfill your destiny The lion, as I mentioned earlier, is meant to confront things, to be courageous and bold, but another very important key you must always remember is that you are never to allow your courage kill your empathy. This is a trap that many people fall into when they start walking on the high places with God. They become so strong, so courageous, that they forget where they came from. They forget the struggles they went through and how people helped them along the way.

The fact that you have become better does not give you the right to match the heads of people or to ignore the sufferings of others. You may have become better than most people, and are now a millionaire, and so there's pride, there's ego, and you think you can just walk on people, but let me warn you, that is a dangerous place to be. It is the same thing as what happened in the Garden of Eden. You were dust, but now you have been lifted and filled with breath within you. And instead of you connecting with the one who gave you the breath, you are listening to a snake who is trying to give you a fruit that is in your own garden. I am warning you, whenever you allow the purpose of synergization with God to be misunderstood, then you are making yourself an enemy of the Most High God, and this is dangerous.

Death In God's House

Have you ever taken time to meditate on the life of Ananias and Sapphira? As soon as they lied when God was creating synergy within the early church do you remember what happened? They sold their land and lied to the apostles in the book of Acts, they did not do it with a pure heart that was synergized with God and the purposes of God. After selling, they lied by bringing just a portion and claiming that was all of it. They wanted people to praise them for being able to give everything, but Peter said, why did you allow Satan to fill your heart to corrupt your synergy with God and the synergy He is creating within the body of Christ? The Bible tells us that both Ananias and Sapphira ended up paying for that error with their lives.

Synergization is serious business my friend, if you want to walk with God and rise with Him, then you must be careful because only when you walk with Him will you experience stability, progress, and achievement. But as you begin to rise with Him and He begins to take you up with Him, you will be so shocked that as wide as His presence can be, it is more difficult to stay up with Him than to stay down.

Down is easy on your shoes, but everyone that went up was told to take off their shoes. Did you hear that? Do you understand what it means to take off your shoes? It's not just about physical shoes. It is about letting go of wrong character and letting go of bad habits. You must become consecrated and set apart for God only. The Bible tells us in Habakkuk 1:13 (KJV), "Thou art of purer eyes than to behold evil, and canst not look on iniquity." So, do you want to synergize with Him on a deeper level? Then get set to let go of everything that is worldly. This is what it means to take off your shoes.

As soon as Moses encountered the burning bush, what was the first thing God said to him? "Take off your shoes." This also means that you have to come to a place where whatever used to be your support system must give way for God and your spiritual covering alone to become your support system. Why? Because at the top, at the deeper levels of your walk, and as you keep rising higher with God, your interactions with spirits will become more intense every day. I am not just talking about angels here, there will also be encounters with terrible spirits that are angry that you made it to the top. Some will even block the gates against you, and you will have to say, "Lift up your heads, O you gates!" Psalm 24:7

This is the reality of walking with God on the high places, it is not for the faint of heart and it is not for those who want an easy life. It is for those who are willing to let go of everything that holds them back, who are willing to face challenges head-on, who are willing to be transformed from the inside out. Are you ready for this deeper level? Are you ready to take off your shoes and walk with God in the high places? The choice is yours, but let me tell you, the view from up there is worth every sacrifice.

Take Away Your Shoes

The Path Of Consecration

You really need to believe this, because if you do not, your pains and your troubles will be in vain. Do you remember Gideon? The Lord called him, and he began to cry about so many challenges, so many problems, and so many foundational and ancestral setbacks in his family lineage. But what did the angel tell him? The angel told him he was a mighty man of valor. Do you not know that you are also a mighty man of valor? It is time to take away your shoes so that you can begin to operate in realms and dimensions that do not make sense to the natural mind and so that the mighty man in you can arise for the world to see. It is time for you to rely on God in greater measure so that your stability, progress, and achievements will come, both in finances, in your health, in your business, even in your spiritual life.

Remember, I said the top in life and in the realm of the spirit is more slippery than being on the ground. However, if you truly take away your shoes and walk in consecration then it will be easier to have a firm grip so that you do not fall. The Bible says in 1 Corinthians 10:12 (KJV), "Wherefore let him that thinketh he standeth take heed lest he fall." If you do not take off your shoes, then you can be sure you will fall. Some people are crying, "Lord, take me to the top in finances!" Hold on, don't you know it is more difficult to be a billionaire than to be average? When you are extremely wealthy, everybody will want a piece of you, they will depend on you and always ask you for things. Also, when you are wealthy, everyone will pretend to be your friend, whereas they are just like Judas, eyeing your millions and also thinking of how to sell you for 30 pieces of silver.

But do not let this discourage you. The path of consecration and of taking away your shoes is about preparing you for these challenges. It is about building your character, strengthening your faith, and aligning your heart with God's purposes. When you are consecrated, when you have truly taken off your shoes, you will be able to handle the pressures and temptations that come with success and wealth. Luke 12:48 (KJV) tells us that "For unto whomsoever much is given, of him shall be much required: and to whom men have committed much, of him they will ask the more." This is why the path of consecration is so crucial; it is this path that will prepare you to be a good steward of the blessings God wants to pour into your life when you arrive the high places.

Taking away your shoes also means stripping away your self-reliance, it means coming to a place where you fully depend on God for everything. Think about it. When you are walking barefoot, you are vulnerable, you feel every pebble, every thorn, every stone on the floor, but that vulnerability makes you more aware, more alert, and more dependent on God to guide your steps so it strengthens your synergization with Him.

I must confess that this path of consecration is not easy, my friend, it will challenge you, and it will stretch you. There will be times when You will want to put your shoes back on and go back to your old and probably corrupt ways of living, but I'm telling you, if you persist and if you stay on this path, You will experience God in unimaginable dimensions of power and glory. You see, when you take away your shoes, when you walk this path of consecration, you are telling God, "I'm all in, I'm not holding anything back. I'm fully surrendered to Your will and Your way." And when God sees that kind of commitment, that kind of surrender, He moves in mighty ways.

One vital thing you should note again in the life of Moses is that when God told Him to take off His shoes because it was a holy ground, it was not the ground that was holy; it was God's presence that made it holy. I said this to reveal to you that when you take off your shoes spiritually, you are positioning yourself to enter

God's presence in deeper ways. And in God's presence, everything changes; Your perspective changes; Your priorities change; Your very nature begins to change; and You start to see things the way God sees them, you start to love what God loves and even hate what God hates. This is the number one essence of walking with God in the high places, it is not just about reaching a certain level of success or achieving certain goals even though all these are important and valid. It is about becoming more like Christ and about allowing God to transform you from the inside out.

Are you ready to take off your shoes? Are you ready to walk the path of consecration? Are you ready to let go of everything that is holding you back and fully surrender to God's will for your life?

God Wants To Reveal His Glory Through You

When you begin to walk in deeper levels with God and successfully take off your shoes, the next thing to know and take very seriously in this world is that God wants to reveal His glory through you. Yes, you heard me right! The God of the universe, the Creator of all things, wants to showcase His glory through your life. So, what does He do? He begins to impact the world through you, and this is another reason you may be facing so many challenges.

He placed salt within you, and that's why He said you are the salt of the earth. He also placed Light within you and then said, you are the light of the world. The benefit of you embracing what God is doing in you and for you is that first, it leads to a turning point for you. When Abraham embraced and entered what God was doing, that was the turning point in his life, but what many people do not realize is that when God raises you as Salt and Light, His mind is so that light will continue to spread across the Earth through you. When God begins to use you, your life begins to operate not just in dual dimensions but in many dimensions, and your light is seen in these ways:

God begins to use your life in giving strength to others: When God begins to reveal his glory through you, you will begin to live a life that is not powered or sponsored by human strength. In fact, when God wants to go somewhere, He will go through you; when He needs to talk to someone, He will talk through you; this is God using your life to bring strength to people in an environment. Always know that somebody is out there who is about to become stronger because of you. Stronger mentally, stronger spiritually, and even physically. So, if you were the devil, would you leave you alone? I am sure the answer is no. So, when everything comes to make you weak, realize that the true intention is never to make you a failure in being used by God.

Think of Samson, for example, every time Delilah asked for the secret of his power and he lied to her, he always destroyed the enemy when they came. But when he gave her the real secret, the enemies came, and his strength was gone. But after a while, what happened? At this time, the enemy must have thought that they had succeeded in crippling him. Never did they know that God still had a restoration plan. So, before we know it, we see Samson's hair growing again. His hair was once again synergizing with his purpose and his call, and by the time it reached a place of strength, the Lord gave him an opportunity to destroy all his enemies and make them pay for what they did to him. Remember, in 40:29-31 the bible tells us that "He giveth power to the faint; and to them that have no might he increaseth strength. Even the youths shall faint and be weary, and the young men shall utterly fall: But they that wait upon the Lord shall renew their strength; they shall mount up with wings as eagles; they shall run, and not be weary; and they shall walk, and not faint." This is the kind of strength God wants to give you, not just for yourself, but so you can strengthen others and be a light in that environment.

Sometimes you may be weak, tired, and broken in life, you may be trying to pray and even unable to pray. But then God brings one right person who gives you a phone call, or one right person who just sends you a text message. It would be foolish for you to just dismiss that person, what you should know is that God is sending you strength through that person.

When you learn to synergize with that strong person, the enemy will never be able to touch you again, because anything coming against you has to come through that strong person. This is the power of synergy. So, whenever God begins to send strong people into your life, you must learn to value it. The Bible says in Matthew 18:19 (KJV), "Again I say unto you, that if two of you shall agree on earth as touching anything that they shall ask, it shall be done for them of my Father which is in heaven." So many people would have been dead, but God provided them with strong people because He knew that on their own, they were no longer strong enough to step into the place of stability, progress, and achievements.

He Uses You as A Beacon of Hope in a Dark World: Another way that God reveals His glory through you in an even more profound way is that He wants to use you as a beacon of hope in a dark world. He wants to use your life as a testimony of His goodness and faithfulness. He wants to reveal His power through your weakness, His wisdom through your decisions, His love through your actions. He wants people to see your life and instead of dying, they will have hope that all is not lost for them yet. Didn't you notice that when God revealed His glory through Moses, the Israelites were set free from slavery? When He revealed His glory through David, a shepherd boy became a king; When He revealed His glory through Paul, the gospel spread throughout the known world. And now, He wants to reveal His glory through you so that you can be the next beacon of hope to our dying world.

But do not forget, for this to happen you must be willing to be a vessel, you must be willing to be molded, shaped, and refined. You must be willing to go through the fire, to endure the challenges, to face the oppositions, because it is through these elements that God prepares you to reveal His glory. 2 Corinthians 4:7 (KJV) captures it beautifully by saying "But we have this treasure in earthen vessels, that the excellency of the power may be of God, and not of us." You are just an earthen vessel my friend, but thank God there is a synergization between you and heavenly treasure within you. And when that treasure shines through you, it is not about you anymore, it is all about God's glory.

You Must Be Careful

When God starts revealing His glory through you, do not be surprised if some people start turning against you, and do not be shocked if you face more opposition than ever before. You see, the enemy knows that when God's glory is revealed through a yielded vessel, lives are changed, strongholds are broken, and the kingdom of darkness suffers loss. But instead of worrying about what the enemy is doing, I want you to focus on what God is doing in you. The Lord will take you places you never dreamed of, He will open doors that were shut tight, and He will make a way where there seems to be no way because when God's glory is on display through you, nothing is impossible. This is the path of true stability, progress, and achievement.

But in all these, you must stay humble, and you must remember that it is not about you, rather it is all about Him. The moment you start thinking it is your own doing, your own strength, your own wisdom, that is when you are in danger of falling and that's when pride will creep in and corrupt your synergization with God. Do you remember what happened to King Nebuchadnezzar? He looked at his kingdom and said, "Is not this great Babylon, that I have built for the house of the kingdom by the might of my power, and for the honor of my majesty?" (Daniel 4:30 KJV). And what happened? God humbled him right there and then. He lost his kingdom, lost his sanity, and became a beast until he learned to give God the glory.

No matter how high God lifts you, never forget that God revealing His glory through you is not just for your benefit. It's for the benefit of those around you, for your community, for your nation, and even for the world. This is why I always tell the Lord, that "Lord I am available for you." When God's glory is revealed through you, it brings hope to the hopeless, healing to the broken, and salvation to the lost. When you walk into a room filled with despair, and the glory of God is radiating through you because you are well synergized, suddenly hope begins to rise and when you speak words of life to someone who has given up while God's glory is flowing through you, suddenly they will find the strength to keep going. When you extend a hand of compassion to someone who has been rejected while God's glory is shining through you, suddenly they experience the love of the Father. This, my friend, is what it means for God to reveal His glory through you. It is not about making you look good, it's about revealing Him as the Almighty to the world, about showcasing His power, His love, His mercy, and His grace to a world that desperately needs it.

CHAPTER FIVE

STRENGTH IN UNITY AND DIVINE COMPENSATION

"Synergization is the bridge from isolation to empowerment; don't let synergy haters pull you into their shadow."

THE DANGERS OF SYNERGY HATERS

When you begin to yoke yourself with a synergy hater, you are treading on treacherous ground, my friend. This is a major reason many people fail the very moment they get married. The instant you intertwine your life with someone who despises synergization, it has a terrible way of depleting your strength, leaving you a mere shadow of your former self. You will suddenly begin to doubt yourself, to loathe your very being, and all manner of negativity will start creeping into your mind like unwelcome parasites.

When two people come together in holy matrimony, it is meant to produce strength, power, and a wellspring of encouragement in your spirit. But have you seen some couples who engage in ceaseless conflict day in and day out? They have failed to understand the power and essence of synergization, and so their lives will forever remain stagnant, never progressing forward or leaving any meaningful imprint on this earth because their divisions will continue to grant the enemy unfettered access to their lives, their children's futures, their business endeavors, and every facet of their existence. "For where envying and strife is, there is confusion and every evil work." (James 3:16, KJV) This scripture shows us the bare consequences of living in a state of constant conflict. When you allow a synergization hater into your life, you are inviting confusion and every form of evil to take root. It's like leaving the gates of your fortress wide open, practically begging the enemy to walk right in and wreak havoc.

Synergy in a relationship is more than just physical proximity or sharing things together, it is a spiritual and emotional alignment that propels each person forward. When couples or even friends lack this understanding, their lives become stagnant, and they lose the power to progress since their actions and decisions will always be hindered because the division between them grants the enemy access to every area of their lives. Look at the Bible in Amos 3:3 (KJV), "Can two walk together, except they be agreed?" This question truly shows that without unity, without synergy, no progress, stability, or achievement can be made can be made.

The dangers of associating with synergy haters go far beyond mere personal inconvenience. These individuals have the potential to derail your entire destiny, to snuff out the flame of your purpose before it has a chance to truly ignite. Think about it, when you are in the company of someone who constantly belittles your dreams, who scoffs at your ambitions, who tries to clip your wings before you can even try to soar, what happens? Your confidence begins to wane, your resolve starts to crumble, and before you know it, you are questioning whether you were ever meant to fly in the first place.

And let us not forget about the impact on those around you. If you are a parent, your children will grow up in an environment devoid of unity and mutual support. They will learn to view relationships as battlegrounds rather than partnerships, thereby perpetuating a cycle of discord that could span generations. Once you have identified someone as a synergy hater, you need to make some tough decisions. Do not forget that not everyone is meant to journey with you to your promised land, some people are just passing through, and others need to be left behind at the departure lounge of your destiny. It might be painful, it might be difficult, but sometimes, you must cut ties with those who are hindering your progress because they do not value synergizations.

Instead, surround yourself with synergy lovers, seek people who understand the power of unity, who are willing to work together towards a common goal, who will challenge you to be better, and simultaneously support your growth. These are the people who will help you soar to new heights, who will stand with you in times of trouble, and who will celebrate your victories as if they were their own.

Guard your heart my friend, guard your relationships, and guard your synergizations with God and with the men he has ordained to be part of your destiny. Do not let the synergization haters rob you of your strength, your joy, and your very destiny.

God's Compensation Of Your Weakness

When God wants to compensate for your weakness, He does not always just bestow strength upon you like some magical endowment. No, sometimes, in His infinite wisdom, He gives you strong people to synergize with. It is as if He is saying, "My child, I see your struggles, I understand your limitations, and I'm sending you reinforcements in human form."

Think about the early church, as recorded in the book of Acts, after the apostles were attacked, flogged, and beaten, the Bible tells us that they immediately went into their own company and prayed for boldness. Acts 4:23-24 (KJV) says, "And being let go, they went to their own company, and reported all that the chief priests and elders had said unto them. And when they heard that, they lifted up their voice to God with one accord..." They did not retreat into isolation to lick their wounds. No, they went straight into their own company, their circle of fellow believers, and there they prayed for boldness. Now, why do you suppose they had such a company? Why did they instinctively run to their own people in times of trouble? It is because that gathering was a place of synergization, a circle where they could combine their efforts, pool their faith, and draw strength from one another.

Verse 31 then tells us "And when they had prayed, the place was shaken where they were assembled together; and they were all filled with the Holy Ghost, and they spake the word of God with boldness." This scripture clearly shows us the power of synergized prayer and the strength that comes from godly synergizations. The very ground beneath their feet trembled in response to their collective supplication, and they emerged from that gathering filled with the Holy Spirit, emboldened to continue their mission despite the threats they faced.

In Matthew 18:20 we read "For where two or three are gathered together in my name, there am I in the midst of them." This was our Lord Jesus Himself showing us the importance of coming together in Synergization, He gives us an assurance that when we gather His presence is always there. This is God trying to let you know that you must take church seriously, because the body of believers are available to be strong men of compensation for you as you go through the journey of life. In light of this divine strategy, you must learn to value and respect the strong individuals God has positioned around you. They are not there by mere chance or coincidence, they are there by divine appointment, strategically placed to compensate for your areas of weakness and to provide the support you need to fulfill your God-given purpose.

But here is where many of us miss the mark, we are so focused on our own self consumed by our personal struggles, that we do not recognize the strength God has placed at our disposal through others. We are like a man dying of thirst while floating on a vast ocean, not realizing that salvation is quite literally all around us. Open your eyes, my friend! Look around you. Those strong people in your life, they are not there to intimidate you or make you feel inadequate, they are there to complement you, to fill in the gaps where you are lacking, and to be the hands and feet of God's compensating grace in your life so synergize with them quickly

Also, aside from valuing the strong people around you, you must also learn to let the weak people in your circle tap into your own strength. Yes, you heard me right. It is a two-way street, Just as God used others to compensate for your own weakness, He will also use you to compensate for the weakness of others. There are certain people in your sphere who do not believe in themselves, who cannot see their own potential. Why don't you believe in them? When they can't envision a future for themselves, be their eyes and illuminate the path ahead, don't make the grave mistake of trampling on the weak people around you as you ascend to new heights, and don't become so enamored with the growth of your own hair that you forget to help others tend to theirs.

Let us go back to the story of Samson for a moment, when his hair began to grow back, signaling the return of his strength, how did he destroy the enemy? He had to synergize with a young child. It is as if he was saying, "I've been praying for this moment for so long, and now my hair is back, but I need your eyes to guide me." Do you think he would have ever been able to accomplish his final act of redemption on his own? Not a chance! So, you see, you cannot do everything by yourself, you must value the people God brings into your life and synergize with them because they are His compensation for your weaknesses on the path to fulfilling your destiny.

Learn to Ask God for Help, Wisdom, and Compensations When Needed

In James 1:5 the bible says, "If any of you lack wisdom, let him ask of God, that giveth to all men liberally, and upbraideth not; and it shall be given him." But here's the catch, you must ask boldly, believe Him wholeheartedly, and banish all second thoughts from your mind. For many people, their doubts and reservations are the very reasons they are not seeing results. Their second thoughts are eroding their synergy with the Lord, creating static in the divine connection that is meant to empower them. Anything that disrupts your focus when synergy is supposed to be created is your Delilah, and you must fight against it with every fiber of your being. I have never encountered anything that sabotages synergization like the deception of multiple options. What makes synergy truly effective is when you act as though you have no other choice but to trust in God's provision and the strength He provides through others.

Playing nice before the big shots of this world and defiling yourself with worldly compromises is not an option when you want to stand before God in the high places of spiritual authority. You cannot keep standing on the fence, saying, "Well, I'm a Christian, but I'm not all that religious." That, my friend, is a statement of spiritual lukewarmness that has no place in the life of a true believer. You must consecrate yourself wholly to the Lord, and then embrace only the strength He provides both directly and through the people He has placed in your life. Do not forget, in God's economy, nothing is wasted, your weaknesses are opportunities for His strength to be perfected, your strengths are meant to be shared, to lift up others who are struggling. When we fully understand and embrace this divine synergy, we become unstoppable forces for God's kingdom with each of us playing our part in God's universal and ultimate plan.

Don't Live Anyhow

Search For The Opportunities God Is Providing

Whether you realize it or not, the enemy sees you as an object of mockery, and he constantly seeks ways to belittle and humiliate you. He does this not just to amuse himself, but also to hinder you from fulfilling your God-given potential. But here is what you need to understand, whenever you notice that mockery in your life is intensifying, that is a sign that something is growing inside you, something powerful. Whether it is spiritual, financial, emotional, or even ministerial mockery, it is a sign that a new season of greatness is on the horizon. But you must be careful. The devil's goal is to blind you with your current challenges so you cannot appreciate or even notice the wonderful things God is doing in your life. He wants you angry at God, so you will remain stagnant.

But instead of succumbing to despair, it is time to search for the opportunities God is providing. In Judges 16:25-27 (KJV), the bible shows us that Samson's enemies paraded him out and brought him to their midst, intending to make a spectacle and mockery of him. But I want you to see beyond the surface of this narrative. I want you to recognize the opportunities that God is continually providing, even in the midst of hopeless circumstances. Sometimes, these divine openings may not appear particularly appealing or promising, but you must understand that God is guiding you toward your place of ultimate victory. They were unaware that his hair was beginning to grow back, symbolizing his return to strength. They thought they had defeated him, but God had other plans. Just like Samson, when you find yourself in situations where it seems like the world is mocking you, understand that your "hair", your strength, your purpose, and your destiny is growing back. Do not let the enemy deceive you into thinking that your situation is hopeless. The Bible says in Isaiah 40:31 (KJV), "But they that wait upon the Lord shall renew their strength; they shall mount up with wings as eagles; they shall run, and not be weary; and they shall walk, and not faint."

This is the time to regain your God-confidence, your self-confidence, and your hunger for purpose. Even if it seems like nothing significant is happening in your life, look for those little passions that make you want to live, that make you want to fight for your destiny. God is working in the background, and He is bringing you closer to your victory, even if the path does not seem clear right now. God used a mere child to assist Samson in his final act of redemption. He employed a young girl to direct Naaman to the place where he could find healing. What I am trying to impress upon you is that the Almighty can use anyone, regardless of their age, status, or apparent capabilities to help you along your journey. The key is to achieve synergization with them and to place your trust in God as well as to internalize the truth that you can never truly go it alone in this life.

Samson did not tell the boy what his plan was because if he had, the boy would have unintentionally revealed his intentions to the Philistines. Likewise, you need to be careful about who you share your plans and dreams with. Use discernment and wisdom to identify who is mature enough to handle the weight of your vision and always never forget that not everyone will understand your purpose. Yes, some will even sabotage it, whether intentionally or unintentionally.

In this season of your life, you cannot afford to live carelessly. You must be intentional about every step you take, every word you speak, and every decision you make. Your destiny is too important to be left to chance and this is why you must always seek clarity from God and position yourself with His will. If you are not sure where to start, go back to the basics. What has God already said to you? What passions has He placed in your heart? What doors has He already opened? When you begin to focus on these things, you will start to see the opportunities God is providing, even in the midst of mockery and challenges.

I challenge you today, my friend, to open your spiritual eyes wide. Look beyond the surface of your circumstances, that difficulty you are currently grappling with, It might just be the doorway to your destiny, that person who seems insignificant or bothersome. They might be carrying the very key to unlock your next level of breakthrough. Do not live your life haphazardly, drifting along with no clear direction or purpose. Instead, live with intentionality, with your spiritual antenna constantly attuned to the movements of God in your life. For He is always at work, orchestrating events and circumstances for your ultimate good, even when you cannot see or understand His methods.

Surround yourself with individuals who will support your vision, who will pray with you and for you, and who will believe in you even when you struggle to believe in yourself. But always remember to guard your heart and your vision, being wise as serpents and harmless as doves in your interactions with others.

CHAPTER SIX

THE PATH OF TRUE STABILITY

"Storms will come, but a heart anchored in faith will never be swayed by the winds of adversity."

YOU ARE CALLED TO BE RELIABLE

Has it ever occurred to you that being tall is useless if you are not strong, being strong is useless if you cannot stand, and standing is useless if you are not firm. Today, I want you to know that God is calling you and me to a place of reliability and stability, a place where we can be counted upon to stand firm in the face of adversity and to be the pillars of strength that others can lean on in times of trouble. This calling is not for the faint of heart, but for those who are willing to embrace the challenges that come with being a dependable servant of the Most High. Please understand this truth, there are those in the kingdom of God who are liabilities, these are the individuals who instead of contributing to the growth and strength of the Body of Christ are draining its resources and hindering its progress.

But then what is the solution? The cure for being a liability, the antidote to this spiritual malaise, is to become reliable. "It is reliability that exempts you from being a liability," that transforms you from a burden into a blessing. And this should matter to you because every aspect of human life, every interaction, every relationship, every endeavor, depends on someone who is reliable, someone who can be trusted to follow through on their commitments and stand firm in their convictions.

You might say, with a dismissive wave of your hand, "Oh, I will never get married," but you want a job, right? If you have a job but you are not reliable, who will keep you? Nobody. No employer in their right mind would keep an employee who cannot be counted on to show up, to complete their tasks, or to contribute positively to the workplace. Or you say, with a touch of cynicism, "I don't want to have children because it's too much work," but you want a husband. What kind of husband, I ask you, will stay with an unreliable woman? A man of integrity, a man of God, seeks a partner who is steadfast, who can be depended upon in both the mundane tasks of daily life and the crucial moments that define a relationship.

The same principle applies to the fairer sex, what good wife, what virtuous woman of God, will stay with an unreliable man? A man who cannot be trusted to provide, to protect, to lead his family in the ways of the Lord. You want a business, you want a good life, but who will continue to do business with an unreliable person, unless they too are unreliable? In the world of commerce, reliability is the currency that builds trust, that forges lasting partnerships and separates successful entrepreneurs from those who falter and fail.

In my country, we have a saying on this matter "Cunny man die, cunny man bury am." You see, con men are drawn to each other like moths to a flame, each trying to outsmart the other, each believing they are the cleverest person in the room. But in the end, they are just playing each other, trying to be smart, but ending up becoming useless, their lives are a cautionary tale of deceit and emptiness. Everything in this world, everything of value, everything that lasts, works on the foundation of reliability. It is the bedrock upon which all meaningful relationships and successful endeavors are built.

The reason we serve Jesus, the very foundation of our faith, is because He is reliable, and this is why synergization with Him is also powerful. When all else fails, when the world turns its back on you, when friends forsake you and family misunderstands you, you can always be sure that you can count on Jesus. He is the same yesterday, today, and forever, a constant source of strength and comfort in our ever-changing world. God wants you to be stable, to emulate this divine reliability in your own life. And by the grace of God, I stand on the authority of His Word and pray for you, believing for a miraculous transformation in your life in Jesus' name.

I declare that the spirit of instability that has entered your bones, making your joints weak and your resolve feeble, will be driven out in Jesus' name! In our world today, so many people look like they are standing and act reliable, however, they are just putting on a facade of dependability for the world to see, but deep within, in the secret chambers of their heart, they are undependable. They are unreliable, tossed back and forth by every wind of doctrine and every temptation that comes their way. But Jesus, the Great Physician, the Healer of our souls, will fix you just in case you are in this category, I pray that He will perform the spiritual surgery needed to transform you from the inside out in Jesus' name.

If it is your eyes that need healing because they are clouded by the distractions of this world, He will do it, restoring your spiritual vision to clearly see the path He has set before you. If it is your heart that needs mending, hardened by disappointment and betrayal, He will do it, softening it and making it beat in rhythm with His own. If it is your ears that need opening, deafened by the noise of this world, He will do it, tuning them to hear His still, small voice. If it is in your knees, weakened by the burdens you have been carrying, He will do it, strengthening them so you can stand firm and unshakable. Even in your marrow, in the very core of your being, I pray that He will infuse you with His divine strength and stability.

Be Aware of Yourself and Your Weaknesses

All the deception that Satan uses, the high waves of water he uses to threaten you, making you think those waves are more powerful than the dependability of Jesus Christ, by God's power and by the reason of this service, I command those satanic activities and demonic distractions in your life to be exposed, destroyed, and defeated in the name of Jesus! No longer will you be swayed by the storms of life; no longer will you be intimidated by the roaring waves of adversity. You will stand firm, anchored in the unshakeable reliability of Christ.

The blindness that Satan put in your mind is the same he put in Peter's. Peter was so sure, so confident in his own strength, that he declared, "Me? Jesus, never! I will never leave you!" Even when Jesus, in His divine omniscience, told him, "Peter, I know you. I see you, I know everything," Peter still argued, still and clung to his misplaced self-confidence. Some people argue out of pretense, out of deceit, their words are like a smokescreen to hide their true intentions, but others, like Peter, argue out of ignorance because they are unaware of the weaknesses lurking in their own hearts.

Peter was arguing out of ignorance, his words were fueled by a misplaced zeal rather than true understanding. He even boldly said "Lord, if everyone leaves you, I will never deny you,", his voice was ringing with sincerity but in reality, the Lord knew he would not be able to stand the temptation when the deal day comes.

As a child of God reading this today, I want you to know that the next shining stars in the kingdom will be reliable Christians. They may not have all the drama and noise, and they may not draw attention to themselves with grand gestures and loud proclamations but they will have something far more valuable, something God can count on; and that thing they will have is reliability, their faith will not a fleeting emotion but a steadfast commitment to our heavenly father. They are people who their bones are strong, their marrow is healthy, and their entire being is fully in synergization and properly in alignment with the purposes of God. These are not people trying to showcase themselves, to build their own kingdoms, or establish their own reputations. No, they are showcasing Jesus, every action, every word, every thought from them is aimed at glorifying their Savior and advancing His kingdom.

Everything they do is aimed at getting closer to Jesus, deepening their relationship with Him, and drawing men back to Him because they know with unshakeable certainty that if they are close to Jesus they will be relevant in everything He is doing. Therefore, they become the ones who give others a fresh start, a new beginning, pointing the way to redemption and restoration. Concisely, they lift people up, they do not sink them, and they do not tear others down to build themselves up.

This is the kind of person I have made up my mind to be every day of my life and I am inviting you into this lifestyle also. I do not sink people, I lift people, I do not destroy things, I build things. I only destroy satanic things and those seeking to spoil the kingdom of Christ. This is the calling of every one of us as a believer, it is a call to be an agent of change in this world, to be a force for good in this world, and to be a beacon of hope in the darkness and a reliable representative of Christ in a world that is desperately in need of stability and the truth of God.

Your Cry Every day

Your cry every day should be Oh God, make me strong, make me firm, make me immovable, unshakable. Make me firm! Lord. This should be the cry of every believer's heart, a passionate plea for divine empowerment to stand firm in the face of adversity. 1 Corinthians 15:58 says it like this "Therefore, my beloved brethren, be you steadfast, unmoveable, always abounding in the work of the Lord, forasmuch as you know that your labour is not in vain in the Lord."

I repeat it again for you by the Spirit of God "Reliable people are the next brightest stars in God's kingdom." Child of God if you notice that God is being hard on you in an unusual way, cutting off certain things, severing negative soul ties, demanding a deeper commitment, and drawing you closer, I want you to know that it's because He is calling you to a higher place, He is preparing you for greater responsibilities and equipping you to be a pillar of strength in His kingdom.

Follow God's Script And Path For Your Life

Moses was on the ground when he saw the burning bush, a humble shepherd tending his flock in the wilderness, but God had greater plans for him, plans that would require him to climb over 7,600 feet up to that place, at the age of 80! Can you imagine the physical and mental fortitude needed for such a journey? And yet, you tell an 18-year-old to do something, and they say, "I'm tired." Yes, I understand tiredness, the weariness that comes from the daily grind of life, but Moses, despite his advanced age and the difficulty of the task before him, still went up to the mountain of God, answering the divine call with unshakable obedience. And now, 4,000 years later, we are still talking about him because his story a testament to the power of reliability and obedience to God's call. Over 3,000 years have passed, and the world is still talking about him, his name has become synonymous with leadership, faith, and divine encounter. Even 7,000 years from now, long after our names have faded from memory, the world will still be talking about Moses and his legacy as an enduring inspiration to all who seek to follow God with their whole hearts.

I want you to understand and to catch this with every fiber of your being, that you are an actor in the movie of God. Your life is not a random series of events, not a meaningless struggle against fate. No, you are part of a grand narrative, a divine screenplay written by the Author of life Himself. The Lord is saying to you with tender authority today, "Allow Me to write the script of your life, and make sure you follow My script." This is not a suggestion, not a polite request, but a divine imperative. If you follow His script, if you get to the place of synergization between your will and His will, you will win. You will triumph over every obstacle, overcome every challenge, and fulfill the glorious purpose for which you were created.

"He brought me up also from a horrible pit and set my feet on a rock to stand. He put a new song in my mouth to sing." These words from the Psalmist in Psalm 40:2 captures the transformative power of following God's script to rule in your life. It is gratitude, a heart overflowing with thanksgiving, that will help you overcome the trauma of your horrible pit experiences and when you focus on God's goodness, on His faithfulness in bringing you out of the miry clay, you will find the strength to stand firm and to sing a new song of victory and praise.

You see, before God parted the Red Sea before the Children of Israel, it looked like a terrible situation and an insurmountable obstacle that would spell doom for the Israelites, but when they crossed the Red Sea, walking on dry ground between walls of water, God allowed the enemy to get close. Isn't it amazing? Why would He do this? Why would He allow the enemy to get so close and even enter the same water? The Bible says it was because God wanted to use that same water to overthrow the enemy! This means the very challenges you walked through, the very trial that was designed to destroy you, is what will eventually be the instrument of your enemy's defeat.

The book of Hebrews 11:29 tells us that by faith, the Israelites walked through the Red Sea on dry ground because God gave them a chosen leader, but when the enemy tried to do the same thing, they failed miserably, their chariots and horsemen were swallowed up by the returning waters. So, standing firm among several things means finding God's path, discerning His will for your life, and following it with full commitment. Child of God, it's time to find God's designated path for your victory, because it is on this path that you will find the strength to overcome every obstacle and emerge victorious in life and do you know what? God is counting on you!

God has Great Plans for You!

Psalm 16:11 "Thou wilt show me the path of life; in Your presence is fullness of joy, and at Your right hand, pleasures forevermore." This promise from the Psalms is an assurance for us that God will reveal His path to us, and that He will guide us into the fullness of life that He has prepared for us. You must find that designated path, God has prepared it for you, and He will show it to you in His perfect timing. The key is to remain in His presence, to cultivate a lifestyle of intimacy with Him, for it is in His presence that we find not only direction but also the strength to walk in that direction. And when you begin to follow God's directions your enemy cannot follow you, if they do, they will be destroyed. This is why when the Egyptians tried to follow the same path through the Red Sea, God discomfited their chariots. And as their chariots failed, the Israelites continued to move forward, just as you will continue to move forward in stability, progress, and eventually achieve destiny as long as you are synergized with the Lord. By the time the Egyptians realized their grave error, it was a futile effort. The Bible says they decided to turn back, to flee from the presence of the God of Israel. But it was too late, the waters that had parted for God's people now came crashing down upon their pursuers.

Now, I say to you, and I declare with divine authority that every enemy that has been chasing you, has been set up by God! You thought you were running, fleeing in fear and desperation, but God was using you to set a trap for the enemy! And now, by the power of the Holy Ghost, every enemy that has been chasing you will turn back and run. They will flee, but it will be too late. God will swallow them up, defeat them, and destroy them in the name of Jesus!

Hebrews 12:2 says we are to keep our eyes on Jesus, the author and finisher of our faith. This means we are to look away from the natural realm, from the circumstances that threaten to overwhelm us and fasten our gaze on Jesus, who birthed faith within us and who leads us forward into faith's perfection. So, faith has to be birthed within you, a divine implantation of trust and confidence in God. But it does not end there, it is a journey, a lifetime process of growth and maturation so do not think the victory is complete once faith is birthed, rather realize that it is just the beginning point, and it is a great sign that God is doing so much with you. However, you must stay with Him and continue in synergization until that faith that is birthed becomes perfected and refined in the fires of God and emerges as pure gold.

Stay Focused!

As we continue to travel with God following His script for our lives, I want you to never forget Hebrews 12:2 which says "We look away from the natural realm and we fasten our gaze onto Jesus who birthed faith within us and who leads us forward into faith's perfection. His example is this: Because his heart was focused on the joy of knowing that you would be his, he endured the agony of the cross and conquered its humiliation, and now sits exalted at the right hand of the throne of God!" (Passion Translation)

Can you see it, the Bible says we are to follow His example, **_"Because His heart was focused."_** You cannot be firm if you are easily distracted, you cannot be firm if you are eventually distracted, and then there is a third group of those who are systematically distracted.

The systematically distracted are the most terrible ones because these are the ones who know God. They know His ways and are committed, at least on the surface. Satan knows they will never turn their backs on God openly, so he creates a system to slowly pull them away. He creates distractions that do not seem dangerous at first, but over time, they will lead them away from

God's purpose. These distractions are most times subtle, a slight compromise here, a small indulgence there, but over time, they will destroy the foundation of faith and reliability that God is seeking to build in these people's life.

I want you to read Romans 8:38-39, and make up your mind that you will never be carried away by the enemy's distractions "For I am persuaded, that neither death, nor life, nor angels, nor principalities, nor powers, nor things present, nor things to come, Nor height, nor depth, nor any other creature, shall be able to separate us from the love of God, which is in Christ Jesus our Lord."

Don't Fail God

No matter what you do in life you must endeavor to see that you never fail God. Do you remember when Jesus was on trial, arrested, and being taken away, this was the culmination of God's divine plan which was set in motion even before the foundation of the world.

The first thing Satan took advantage of which he did not create was the cold, a cold that was affecting those who waited in the courtyard. The second thing that he did not create but also took advantage of was the fire, a source of warmth that drew people together, creating an environment ripe for confrontation and temptation because if you are cold, you will naturally seek warmth, from the fire. But what Satan really used was the people, he did not create them, but he positioned them strategically to challenge Peter's core beliefs and to shake the very foundation of his faith.

Before Peter even realized what was happening, a young girl spoke up, questioning him and harassing him with relentless interrogation about Jesus. Before he knew it, someone else spoke up, and then another. At this point, his very core, the foundation of who he was, and his identity as a follower of Christ came under attack. That is what we call systematic distraction. It is where Satan distracts you, but you may not even realize He is pulling you down until it is too late and until you find yourself in a pit of denial and despair. Who would have thought Peter, the bold and confident Peter, the rock upon who caught the revelation of Christ as the Son of God, would be swearing and denying that he ever knew Jesus? But there he was, his voice rising in desperation and saying, "I don't know the man!" It's possible you may be in that position now, a position where your faith is being tested by trials, challenges, sins, and many other things, this is the greatest time to strengthen your synergization with the Lord if you want to remain stable and on the path of progress and achievement.

At that moment, when all seemed lost, the Bible says God used a rooster to remind Peter. The sound of that rooster crowing pierced through the night and the fear that had clouded Peter's mind, and suddenly, Peter remembered the prophecy of Jesus "Before the rooster crows, you will deny me three times." With a shattered heart, Peter then went out, weeping bitterly and full of remorse and regret. Now, imagine if Peter had never entered the courtyard. Perhaps he would not have fallen, and he would not have experienced the crushing guilt of denying his Lord. But he also would have failed in the area of his commitment, where he said with such bravado, "I will stay with you, Lord." But at the end of it all, John was there, John followed, John stayed and John watched Jesus being beaten, his heartbreaking but his faith unshaken. John was there when Jesus hung on the cross, a witness to the greatest act of love the world has ever known. This is why Jesus could looked at John and said, "Behold your mother. Mother, behold your son." And from that moment, John took care of her.

When you look at all this, it is many times easy to miss Luke 22:54 (KJV): "Then took they him, and led him, and brought him into the high priest's house. And Peter followed afar off." Do you see that?

Peter followed from afar, this was where his problem started, to follow from afar symbolically for many of us today, will mean "backsliding". Following from afar is proof that his synergization was no longer as strong as it should be and that he was already losing reliability and stability. And by the time he entered the temple, he was gone, lost to the distraction, swept away by the tide of fear and self-preservation

Now here is the point that I want to drive home to your hearts, as believers we cannot afford to fail God by losing our frontliners to systematic distractions. We cannot! The body of Christ needs its warriors, its champions of faith, we need them to stand firm on the front lines of spiritual battle so we must engage in fervent and unceasing intercessions to overturn these satanic distractions and we must stand in the gap for our brothers and sisters, lifting them up before the throne of grace, praying for strength and steadfastness in the face of temptation every day.

Don't fail God, beloved, He is counting on you to be his hand and his light in this dark world, to be a pillar of strength when others are shaking, to be a voice of truth when lies abound because you have been called to be reliable, to be steadfast and to be immovable through the power of synergization. And although the path may be difficult, though the challenges may seem insurmountable, remember that you do not walk alone, the God who you have synergized with is called faithful, and He will equip you for every good work. Until stability, progress, and achievement become the testimony of every area of your life, both physically and spiritually

CHAPTER SEVEN

SYSTEMATIC DISTRACTIONS OF BITTERNESS AND INGRATITUDE

"An open heart is the gateway to divine revelation so guard against negativity that builds walls around your spirit."

THE DANGER OF INGRATITUDE AND BITTERNESS

T he Bible, in its infinite wisdom, provides us with a powerful illustration of the consequences of ingratitude and bitterness in the book of Numbers 14:11 (KJV), where the Lord speaks to Moses, "And the Lord said unto Moses, How long will this people provoke me? and how long will it be ere they believe me, for all the signs which I have shewed among them?" This verse sets the stage for understanding the gravity of the Israelites' situation and the disappointment God felt towards their constant complaining and lack of faith in Him as their God. Psalm 106:24-25 (KJV) tells us "Yea, they despised the pleasant land, they believed not his word: But murmured in their tents and hearkened not unto the voice of the Lord."

The Passion Translation (TPT) Captures it this way "They despised the land of delight you gave to them. They did not believe your promise or rely on your word. They grumbled and found fault with everything and closed their hearts to your voice" This verse is showing us a clear picture of a people so consumed by their own negativity that they failed to recognize the blessings bestowed upon them by the Almighty.

Their grumbling was not merely a sign of dissatisfaction; it was an indicator of ingratitude, a dangerous symptom of spiritual backsliding that we must guard against with every fiber of our being. You see, when your heart is right, you will find yourself naturally inclined to see the good in every situation, no matter how challenging it may appear on the surface. It is like having a pair of divine spectacles that allow you to perceive the hidden blessings in even the most trying circumstances. But when your heart is wrong or filled with bitterness you will find fault in everything. And let me tell you, once you start on this path of finding fault in everything, it will inevitably slip into every aspect of your life, you will find fault in your relationships, you will find fault with your children, with your spouse, your friends, your colleagues at the office, I mean nobody will be spared.

And when there is no one else left to blame, when you have exhausted all external targets for your blame, you will turn that harsh and unforgiving spirit of faultfinding towards your own self. You will start finding faults with yourself, with your decisions, your actions even every thought until you are left feeling utterly inadequate and unworthy. But make no mistake, this is nothing, but a cleverly disguised deception orchestrated by the enemy of our souls!

Strive To Maintain an Open Heart

The devil, in his cunning and wicked ways wants nothing more than to distract you from the abundant life God has planned for you so He will employ all these tactics of ingratitude and bitterness to keep you either anxiously chasing after the high waves of worldly pursuits or being relentlessly pursued by the high waves of your own negative emotions. It is a lose-lose situation designed to keep you off balance, unstable, and far from the peace and joy that come from a heart synergized with God. So, God is saying to you, the best gift you can receive from Him is the gift of stability. When you read that verse again you will see they grumbled and found fault with everything, and what happened? They closed their hearts to your voice." It is like they put up a 'Do Not Disturb' sign on their hearts, shutting out the very voice of God that was supposed to guide them, comfort them, and lead them to the promised land.

I have told you before, if it is hard for you to hear God, to see, or to connect with the spirit realm, it is not God's fault. You might think, "But my heart is open!" No, your heart is closed. Grumbling and complaining are signs of a closed heart, it is like you are building a wall of negativity brick by brick, and with each complaint, that wall gets higher and thicker, making it harder for God's voice to get through to you. How do we know your heart is open? It is revealed through the abundant revelation that comes to you, but unfortunately, for some people, it doesn't matter if they don't hear God's voice, the devil has deceived them into thinking they don't need to hear God and that they can live life on their own, what a shame! But it should matter to you! The voice of God is the golden key to a stable life, it is like having a spiritual GPS, guiding you through the twists and turns of life with pinpoint accuracy.

When you keep reading 106: from verse 26 (TPT) The bible says, "So you gave up and swore to them that they would all die in the desert." (I pray that this will not be your portion in Jesus' name.) And you scattered their children to distant lands as exiles. Then our fathers joined in worship of false gods named Lord of the Pits. They even ate the sacrifices offered to the dead. Their actions made you burn with anger, so much so that a plague broke out among them until Phinehas intervened and executed the guilty, causing judgment to fall upon them. Because of this act of righteousness, Phinehas will be remembered forever."

Can you Phinehas, because of his actions the word of God tells us that he will be remembered forever, I promise you, there is no effort of yours in establishing God's kingdom that will be forgotten.

Be Careful as A Leader (The Error of Moses)

Psalm 106:32 TPT version then continues by saying "Your people also provoked you to wrath at the stream called Strife." This is where Moses got into serious trouble. Even as a leader, you must watch so that the people you are leading do not mislead you. Moses missed the promised land because of the people he was leading there. This is what we call "systematic distraction" where you used to be the encourager but now you are bitter and refuse encouragement because the people were rebellious against you.

Moses exploded in anger and spoke to them out of his bitterness. But here is the lesson, if you are going to be a successful frontliner, you must never allow bitterness to find a resting place in your heart or soul. When you are doing anything for the Lord, do not let the high waves provoke bitterness. When people offend you, fight against bitterness at all costs and never allow it to take root in your heart because bitterness will make you weak, unstable, and irrelevant. It will make you lose everything you have labored for. That is why no matter what I do, I will never speak out of bitterness, if I feel the need to say something, I always ensure my feelings are under control, and that my anger is under control before I speak. As a person I have decided in my heart and in my life never to allow the work I am doing for the Lord to separate me from the Lord of the work.

Now, let's turn our attention to verse 34, for it contains a warning that is particularly relevant to our times: "Neither did our fathers destroy the enemies in the land as you had commanded them; but they mingled themselves with their enemies and learned to copy their works of darkness." Oh, how we need to heed this warning in our day and age!

A Prophetic word

Watch out for mingling, beloved! I have spoken about this before in a Prophecy that the Lord gave me (2024), and I will speak about it again because the danger is real and present. Agents of darkness who have been fed with blood, and I am not speaking in metaphors or giving out conspiracy theories here, these agents are out in the world now, and their spirits are angry, volatile, dangerous. They possess abilities that defy natural explanation, able to change their form at will, manifesting as male or female as it suits their purposes.

I do not say these things to frighten you, but to prepare you for the reality we face. In times past, certain beliefs were prevalent that now seem like superstitions. When Thomas, in his doubt, declared, "Unless I see Jesus, I will not believe," he was expressing a sentiment many of us can relate to. But when Jesus appeared, He did not rebuke Thomas for his doubt. Instead, He invited him to look, to touch, to verify for himself, saying, "Look at me; I am Jesus." He even encouraged Thomas to touch Him, reminding him that "ghosts do not have flesh and bones."

Are you ready for this prophecy?

Those of you who feel weak or vulnerable, I urge you to stand firm in your faith, to clothe yourselves in the full armor of God. And if you find yourself in the company of someone who seems spiritually weak or unstable, exercise caution and discernment. The reality is those who have been consuming human blood and flesh are not just characters in horror stories or urban legends; they walk among us.

This is not a conspiracy theory, my friends. I'm penning this down so that you can listen, learn, and understand the gravity of what we are facing. Often, it is those who think they know everything, those who throw of warnings like these, who end up being the most vulnerable. They quickly become victims of these demonic activities because their skepticism blinds them to the very real danger that surrounds them. In the coming months, you will hear news reports that will shock you, stories of ghostly occurrences and supernatural phenomena that defy logical explanations. When you hear these things, do not be taken aback - it is all part of the end-time reality we are living in.

These entities have the ability to take over the future of a weak person completely, and it goes far beyond what we might think of as simple cloning or identity theft. Hear me clearly: this is the end time. These entities will meet with you; they will share meals with you. If you are not vigilant, if you are not grounded firmly in your faith and protected by the blood of Jesus, you may find yourself caught up in their activities, thinking everything is normal while your very soul is in jeopardy. Before you realize what is happening, you may become what they are, afflicted by a spiritual condition that is almost impossible to reverse. They are already here among us; we are not waiting for their arrival. Joseph, the dreamer in the Bible, understood this kind of threat, he probably warned the people of his town about Herod's intentions to kill every male child, but I am sure many dismissed his concerns, thinking, "What does Herod have to do with us? Our community isn't wealthy; there's been no battle here." But they failed to realize that Herod was driven by a desperate fear, searching for a boy who posed a threat to his throne.

At the end of the day Herod came with bitterness in his heart, trauma in his past, and a paralyzing fear that someone would collect his position. It is a painful reminder that the most dangerous enemies often come not with swords drawn, but with smiles on their faces and poison in their hearts.

As we look around us today, we see many people busily preparing for their future, making plans for 2025 and beyond. But the sad truth is, some of them will not be around to see those plans come to fruition. I say to point out the urgency of our spiritual condition. Many evil people will be removed from this earth, but here is the truly terrifying part: you won't know they are dead because someone - or something - will be using their bodies, mimicking their mannerisms, living their lives as if nothing has changed. I know this sounds like the plot of a science fiction movie, but I assure you, it is the reality we are facing in these last days. That is why it's more crucial than ever to stay alert, to guard your heart against bitterness and ingratitude, and to cling tightly to the truth of God's Word. For it is only in His light that we can see clearly, only in His strength that we can stand firm against the darkness that seeks to engulf us. In conclusion, my beloved, let us take these warnings to heart. Let us cultivate hearts of gratitude, minds renewed by God's Word, and spirits attuned to His voice. For in doing so, we not only protect ourselves from the dangers of ingratitude and bitterness but also position ourselves to be powerful instruments in God's hands, bringing light to a world desperately in need of hope and truth.

Before we round up this chapter and go to the next I will give you a guideline on how you can guard your heart against these destructive forces called bitterness and ingratitude so that bitterness will not prevent you from entering the promised land like Moses and neither will you allow ingratitude to stop you and destroy you like the Israelites. The Bible, in Proverbs 4:23 (KJV), says "Keep thy heart with all diligence; for out of it are the issues of life." This is a bible verse emphasizing the importance of protecting our hearts because it is the wellspring of our actions, attitudes, synergizations with God, and the foundation of stability, progress, and achievements in our lives. Let us now see some essential steps necessary to shield our hearts from anger and bitterness to ensure stability in our lives and walk with God.

Cultivate a Spirit of Gratitude

The first step in guarding our hearts against anger and bitterness is to intentionally cultivate a spirit of gratitude. I am not talking about just saying "thank you" when someone does something nice for you; I am talking about you developing a mindset that sees the good in every situation, no matter how challenging. The Bible tells us in 1 Thessalonians 5:18 (KJV), "In everything give thanks: for this is the will of God in Christ Jesus concerning you." I am not saying this will be easy, especially when life throws you a painful circumstance. But let me tell you, when you start looking for reasons to be thankful, even in the midst of trials, you are building a fortress around your heart that bitterness cannot penetrate. Start each day by counting your blessings no matter how small they may seem and always thank God for the breath in your lungs, the roof over your head, and the people He has placed in your life.

Practice Forgiveness as a Lifestyle

The second step is to make forgiveness a way of life, I know you are thinking "But you don't know what they did to me!" And you are right, I do not. But God does, and He still calls us to forgive. In Ephesians 4:31-32 (KJV) we're instructed to "Let all bitterness, and wrath, and anger, and clamor, and evil speaking, be put away from you, with all malice: And be you kind one to another, tenderhearted, forgiving one another, even as God for Christ's sake hath forgiven you." Forgiveness is not about pretending that what they did was not wrong. It's about releasing the hold that their actions have on your heart and mind when you refuse to forgive, you are the one drinking the poison and expecting the other person to die because bitterness is a heavy burden to carry, and it'll wear you down faster than you can imagine.

Forgiveness is a decision, not a feeling, you might not feel like forgiving, but you can choose to do it anyway.

Renew Your Mind with God's Word

The third step in guarding your heart is to consistently renew your mind with the Word of God. Romans 12:2 (KJV) tells us, "And be not conformed to this world: but be you transformed by the renewing of your mind, that you may prove what is that good, and acceptable, and perfect, will of God." You see, our minds are like gardens and what we plant in them will grow. If you are constantly feeding your mind with negativity, complaints, and worldly perspectives, that is what is going to take root and flourish, but when you fill your mind with God's Word, it acts like a spiritual pesticide, killing off the weeds of bitterness before they can take hold. Therefore, make it a habit to spend time in the Word every day. Do not just read it; meditate on it and let it sink deep into your spirit. When you come across verses about love, forgiveness, and gratitude, do not just skim over them. Stop and really think about what they mean for your life, then ask the Holy Spirit to help you apply these truths to your specific situations.

Surround Yourself with Godly Influences

The fourth step is to carefully choose the company you keep, the bible tells us in Proverbs 13:20 (KJV) "He that walketh with wise men shall be wise: but a companion of fools shall be destroyed." The people you surround yourself with have a very great impact on your attitudes and behaviors. If you are constantly hanging around people who are bitter, complaining, and finding fault with everything, guess what? That negativity is going to rub off on you. But when you surround yourself with people who are full of faith, gratitude, and love for God, their positive attitudes will inspire and encourage you.

Remember, iron sharpens iron so when you are around people who are committed to guarding their own hearts against bitterness, you will find it easier to do the same because they will remind you of God's goodness when you are tempted to focus on the negative, and they will also encourage you to keep pressing forward when you feel like giving up.

Develop a Life of Consistent Prayer and Worship

Another great step in guarding your heart from anger and bitterness is to cultivate a life of consistent prayer and worship. Philippians 4:6-7 (KJV) says "Be careful for nothing; but in every thing by prayer and supplication with thanksgiving let your requests be made known unto God. And the peace of God, which passeth all understanding, shall keep your hearts and minds through Christ Jesus." Prayer is not just about asking God for things; it is about positioning your heart with His heart and when you spend time in His presence, pouring out your heart to Him and listening to His voice, you are creating an atmosphere where bitterness cannot survive. It is like opening the windows of your soul and letting the fresh air of God's love blow through, pushing out all the stale, bitter air.

And worship? Oh, let me tell you about the power of worship! When you lift your voice in praise, even when you do not feel like it, something supernatural happens. Psalm 22:3 (KJV) says that God inhabits the praises of His people. As you worship, you are inviting God's presence into your situation, and in His presence, bitterness and anger melt away like snow in the sunshine. Make it a habit to start and end your day with prayer and worship, also, throughout the day, when you feel anger or bitterness trying to creep in, stop what you are doing and lift up a prayer or sing a worship song, it may feel awkward at first, especially if you are in public, but I promise you, it will change the atmosphere of your heart faster than anything else and keep you very stable.

CHAPTER EIGHT

SYNERGIZATION WITH GOD TAKES YOU BEYOND BEING NORMAL

*Every step towards spiritual synergization
is a step away from weakness*

DO NOT REMAIN CARNAL

No man can really achieve true stability progress and achievements of destiny when you cannot take advantage of synergization to begin living a life that is above normal. Are you set for the ultimate dimensions of stability, progress, and achievements? Then I want you to know that if you remain weak, you will be a victim, if you remain carnal, you will be a victim. Each of us is being called to a higher place and this means you must never joke with your synergization with God! Why get swallowed by the python when you are destined to take over the nations? Does your assignment matter to you enough that the things God wants to accomplish through you become your driving force? Then synergize with Him NOW!

God will empower you; He will build you up! But you must break the wrong synergies you have with the wrong people today. You may be saying, "How do I verify if the people I'm hanging out with are genuine, or perhaps a clone, or even worse, a deceptive spirit?" Let me tell you this, personally I do not live in fear; I live in faith. But if you are living by faith without the power to confront your challenges, you are in trouble. You need the power of God at work in your life so that devils and wrong people will begin to stay far from you.

The Bible warns us that in these days, there will be what we call lying wonders, synergy between politicians and the beast, and false prophets. All these things are coming, so you cannot afford to remain carnal; it will be risky. Many of those who will perish do so because they do not have love for the truth, which could have saved them. If you lack love for the truth and reverence for the Spirit of God, you will fall victim to deceit also. Now, lying wonders should never make you overlook genuine wonders. Instead, let us escalate our pursuit of authentic, living wonders, where we can all go beyond the carnal level, for we will do far better in life and destiny when we carry the true power of God.

Jesus said, "And I will pray the Father, and he shall give you another Comforter, that he may abide with you for ever; Even the Spirit of truth; whom the world cannot receive, because it seeth him not, neither knoweth him: but you know him; for he dwelleth with you, and shall be in you." (John 14:16-17, KJV) This Scripture reminds us of the importance of the Holy Spirit in our lives. He is our Comforter, our guide, and the source of truth. When you remain carnal, you cannot fully receive or understand the Spirit of truth. But when you synergize with God, you will be able to open yourself to His power and wisdom; and through this power and wisdom, you will not only be able to displace the enemy from your life and territory you will also be able to attain exponential stability, progress and great achievements of destiny.

Carnality is A Death Sentence

Romans 8:6 tells us "For to be carnally minded is death; but to be spiritually minded is life and peace." This verse clearly shows us the stark contrast between remaining carnal and pursuing spiritual growth. The carnal mind leads to death, but the spiritual mind brings life and peace. What kind of death are we talking about here? It is death in all dimensions and areas of your life. Carnality will first lead to spiritual death, then physical death, financial death, emotional death, marital death, and death in all areas of your life, do you know why? It is because carnality destroys your synergization affecting your stability, progress, and achievements. This is why we must strive to move beyond our carnal nature and synergize with God.

Now, let me break it down for you further, when I talk about remaining carnal, I am not just talking about indulging in fleshly desires although that is highly inclusive, I am really talking about a mindset that is rooted in the temporal, the earthly, and the self-centered. It is a perspective that is limited by human understanding and devoid of divine insight and power. When you remain at this level, you are an easy prey for the enemy because you are like a sheep without a shepherd, highly vulnerable to every wolf that comes your way. But when you synergize with God, oh my! You tap into a power that's beyond human comprehension. You are no longer operating on your strength, but you are moving in the might of the Almighty. You are no longer limited by your own understanding, but you are guided by the divine wisdom of the All-knowing one. This is why I keep hammering on this point, "you must value synergization!"

Think about it this way, in this natural realm, we all know that a sheep is no match for a wolf. But what happens when that sheep is under the care of a skilled shepherd who understands the art of warfare? The dynamics change completely. The wolf, which once saw an easy meal, now faces a formidable opponent in the shepherd. This is what happens when you synergize with God.

You are no longer an easy target for the enemy, your spiritual life is no longer an easy target, your health is no longer an easy target, your finance is no longer an easy target and you will become a force to be reckoned with.

I've seen what God can do when we move beyond carnality and synergize with Him, and this is why I am very passionate about this message.

Make a decision to break free from carnality today and choose to synergize with God. It may be demanding, but I can also assure you that it will be worth it. The journey may be tough, but the destination is glorious. The process may be painful, but the outcome is powerful. Don't settle for less when God is offering you more. Don't remain a victim when you are called to be a victor. And don't remain stagnant when God is calling you to progress, stability, and wondrous achievements.

You Must Become Discerning In Life

Acts 16:16-18 (KJV) "And it came to pass, as we went to prayer, a certain damsel possessed with a spirit of divination met us, which brought her masters much gain by soothsaying: The same followed Paul and us, and cried, saying, These men are the servants of the Most High God, which shew unto us the way of salvation. And this did she many days. But Paul, being grieved, turned, and said to the spirit, I command thee in the name of Jesus Christ to come out of her. And he came out the same hour."

In this Scripture we just read, a lady was prophesying for many days and proclaiming, "These are men from Hell? These are men from the devil. No! She was prophesying the correct things she said, "These are the great servants of God who show us the ways of the Lord." She kept following the apostles and kept shouting "These men are servants of the great high God, and they are telling us how to be saved." Was she right? Yes, but was she also wrong? Yes. She was both right and wrong because although the information was accurate, the spirit behind it was not.

Everyone who heard her may have thought, "Wow, look at the confirmation from this famous lady in town!" But this is where we must all be cautious. There are many so-called prophets influenced by the spirit of a python. The next verse tells us that day after day she continued to do this until Paul, anointed, turned, and said to the spirit, "I command you in the name of Jesus, to come out of her now!" And what happened? At that very moment, the spirit came out of her. The reaction that followed was significant. The owners, politicians, freemasons, and preachers who had made pacts with demons were furious and immediately sought to destroy Paul, do you know why? It is because they sought to replace Jesus with Satan, as foretold in the Book of Revelation, where the Antichrist will not succeed until the false prophet gives him his power. And it is the exact same things we are experiencing today, the devil has sent his prophets everywhere and they are deceiving the saints, especially those who are still baby Christians. This is why although many Christians are very religious, they are still lacking stability progress and achievements, why? Because they are under the Spirit of a python (divination) and not under the Spirit of a true prophet who can bring them to a place of true synergization with God.

Do not forget that the bible says "Beloved, believe not every spirit, but try the spirits whether they are of God: because many false prophets are gone out into the world." (1 John 4:1, KJV) But it is such a shame that today, believers do not know how to test spirits so they keep mingling themselves with devils, hence they may never see the progress that they desire even if God wants to hand it over to them.

How about Ephesians 5:11 which says, "And have no fellowship with the unfruitful works of darkness, but rather reprove them." This is a bible verse reminding us of our responsibility not only to discern but also to confront and to expose the works of darkness. I know I am called to be a light in today's dark world, and this is why I always speak and prophecy God's world fearlessly and boldly, it's not about me, it is about following the voice of my Lord and shining His light wherever he leads me.

Now, let me break it down for you further so you will not find yourself mingling with devils instead of synergizing with the Lord. Discernment is not about having a good sense of judgment or being able to spot a liar. It is a spiritual gift and a divine ability to see beyond the surface as well as perceive the true nature of things. It's about having spiritual eyes that can see what natural eyes cannot. And let me tell you, in these last days, this gift is more crucial than ever before if you want to be safe, stable, progress, and fulfill your God-ordained destiny. You see, the enemy is cunning, he does not always come at you with blatant evil. Sometimes, he comes disguised as an angel of light and he will begin to use half-truths and twisted scriptures to deceive even the elect if possible. This is why you cannot rely on your natural senses alone. You need spiritual discernment to navigate these treacherous waters. And I declare that your Spiritual antennas will be highly active right now in the mighty name of Jesus.

Consider the lady in our story. On the surface, what she was saying seemed right. She was acknowledging Paul and his companions as servants of God. But Paul, with his spiritual discernment, saw beyond her words and discerned and perceived the spirit behind her utterances, and he knew it was not from God. This is the level of discernment you need to cultivate. It requires a deep and intimate relationship with God, so you can be attuned to His voice, familiar with His, and be able to instantly recognize anything that does not align with His nature. It is like a wife who knows her husband so well that she can tell when someone is impersonating him, even if they get some things right.

Another thing you should know is that discernment operates in the realm of the spirit, its not always logical or easily explainable. Sometimes, you will just have a check in your spirit about a person or situation, don't ignore these promptings! They are the Holy Spirit warning you of danger or deception. Or helping you to recognize the genuine. In today's world which is full of counterfeits, we need to be able to identify and embrace the true move of God and we all need to be able to distinguish between the demonic and the divine or many believers will pay dearly for it with their lives.

Don't Be Scared to Trust Your Spirit

Now, I know you may be thinking, "But what if I make a mistake? What if I discern someone or a situation wrongly?" Well, let me tell you, it is better to err on the side of caution than to blindly accept everything that comes your way. Remember, even the Bereans in the Book of Acts searched the Scriptures daily to verify what Paul was teaching them. And Paul commended them for it! So do not be afraid to question, to verify, and to seek confirmation from the Word and the Spirit.

But here is another thing, discernment without power is dangerous, you may be able to spot the problem, but without the power to confront it, you might still be vulnerable. This is why Paul did not just discern the spirit in that lady; he had the power to cast it out! And this power comes from a deep, intimate relationship with God also. It comes from spending time in His presence, from being filled with His Spirit, and from walking in obedience to His Word. This is another glorious benefit of synergization, when you are synergized with God, you not only have discernment, but you also have authority, and you can speak to situations and see them change. You can confront spirits and see them flee. You become a threat to the kingdom of darkness because you are not just defensive, you are offensive! You are not just avoiding deception, rather you are dismantling it! Yes, this level of discernment and power may attract opposition just like the owners of that slave girl did not just sit back when Paul cast out the spirit. They were furious, they stirred up trouble and you can expect the same. But do you know what, just as no devil was ever able to conquer Paul it is the same way they will never be able to conquer you because you are living in a realm of synergization?

CHAPTER NINE

ENJOYING STABILITY, PROGRESS, AND ACHIEVEMENT

"True victory lies in the art of separation, when you detach from the worldly, you open the door to divine possibilities."

IN SEPARATION LIES YOUR VICTORY

One error that happened with the Israelites is that they mingled themselves with their enemies, unaware that they were learning things that would draw them away from the God who protects them. Before they knew it, they began to serve other gods and bow before idols. This led them away from their purpose, away from their calling, in light of this I am saying to you today do not try to be too smart! If you fail to master the art of separation, you will fall low and if you become mingled with things that seek to intertwine with you, you will become weak, and that weakness will lead to your downfall. 2 Corinthians 6:14 says "Be ye not unequally yoked together with unbelievers: for what fellowship hath righteousness with unrighteousness? and what communion hath light with darkness?"

But what is true Separation? Separation is not about being holier than you or living in a bubble, it is about understanding your identity in Christ and refusing to compromise it, it is about recognizing that you are called to be in the world but not of the world. You have to recognize that when you mingle with the wrong crowd you will unknowingly start adopting worldly philosophies and practices, you are not just risking your personal and spiritual life you are jeopardizing your divine purpose, your stability, your progress, your destiny, and every glorious thing the Lord wants to bring into your life.

The children of Israel were called to be a peculiar people, God's firstborn, and set apart for God's special purposes. But what happened? We saw that they did not understand the necessity of separation, and this led to grievous consequences for them. You may think you are being smart by trying to play with the world a bit, but you are just opening yourself up to corruption. This is why 2 Corinthians 6:17 says "Wherefore come out from among them, and be ye separate, saith the Lord, and touch not the unclean thing; and I will receive you." Just the same way the enemy lured the children of Israel, he still hasn't changed his tactics even today. He is still trying to get God's people and even you to mingle with the world so he can blur the lines between righteousness and unrighteousness, between truth and lies, between divine and demonic. He knows that if he can get ye to compromise a little here, a little there, soon enough, you will find yourself far from where God wants you to be, and that means your progress and glorious destiny have been compromised.

It is high time you master the art of separation by understanding that your uniqueness in Christ is your strength, don't try to fit in with the world, don't try to be like everyone else, instead embrace your peculiarity as a child of God knowing fully well that in separation from the world and synergization with the Lord lies your glorious victory.

Be Prayerful And Empowered

In that story of Paul and the demonic lady, I need you to realize that, yes, the lady had the power to confuse, but Paul had the power to command that spirit out, I said this to reinforce the point I made earlier that as a Child of God, no matter how discerning you are, without the power to cast out demonic forces, whether they be serpents, vipers, vampires, dragons, you will fall victim to them. This is not the time to hide under someone else's power or prayers.

When I say, "Be prayerful," I am not talking about a lukewarm and half-hearted kind of prayer where you just mumble so that people will not say you are not praying. That is a waste of time, and that kind of prayer will not produce the kind of powerful result you are looking for. You must learn to pray violently, with passion and urgency, for power to come! I am talking about a kind of prayer that captures your heart, your soul, and your spirit. Every part of you must be soaked in the fires of a very hot and fervent powerful prayer, especially praying in tongues. In Acts 4, the Apostles had already received power, but when threats came against them, what did they do? They asked for even greater power, and God responded by shaking the ground they stood on. Beloved, I tell you the truth, God's power is necessary to confront the threats of the enemy, especially when your very body, your life, your destiny, your stability, and progress become the target.

Do not be naive! The enemy reacts every time we collapse his agenda, and most times he will try to fight back. But the best way to keep him defeated is to be offensive, to take the battle to the gate, leaving him no chance to retaliate. The apostles prayed for more power, and the Bible says the place where they were gathered shook, and they were all filled with the Holy Spirit, proclaiming the word of God with unrestrained boldness. They prayed for power to heal, to move in signs and wonders, and to boldly face the enemy's threats.

This was not just any kind of prayer or the time for casual and quiet prayers, no, that was not how they prayed. You must pray with everything you have, even if you feel like you are collapsing, keep praying! Pray until power comes! The enemy will use every tool, psychological warfare, financial threats, health issues, and all kinds of things to stop you from praying and even make you doubt God's power, but you must never bow down to Satan.

Read Acts 4:31 for yourself, "And when they had prayed, the place was shaken where they were assembled together; and they were all filled with the Holy Ghost, and they spake the word of God with boldness." (KJV) This Scripture truly shows us the power of fervent and united prayer. When we pray with urgency and faith, God responds powerfully. But you also should note that all prayers are not equal. There is a significant difference between praying and really praying. There's a difference between muttering a few words before you go to bed and engaging in spiritual warfare. The kind of prayer I am talking about is the kind that shakes the foundations of hell, the kind that makes demons tremble, and the kind that moves mountains and parts seas.

The enemy is not playing games, he is out to destroy you, to derail your destiny, to silence your voice. And he will use every trick in his book to do it, he'll attack your mind with doubts and fears, he will attack your body with sickness and disease, he will attack your finances, your relationships, your ministry; and if you are not empowered, if you not "prayed up", you will be an easy target.

This is why I keep hammering on this point "You must be prayerful and empowered!" You cannot afford to be spiritually lazy in these times and you cannot afford to be lukewarm or complacent. The stakes are too high! Your destiny is too important! The souls that God has assigned to ye are too precious!

So how do ye pray like this?

- You need to understand the authority you have in Christ; you are not a beggar approaching God's throne; you are a son, a daughter, with full access to the Father's resources.
- You need to pray with faith, not wishful thinking, but a

deep-rooted confidence in God's ability and willingness to answer.

- You need to pray with persistence, do not give up if you do not see results immediately. Keep knocking, keep seeking, keep asking.
- Always pray in the Spirit by allowing the Holy Spirit to guide your prayers, interceding through you with groanings that words cannot express.
- And finally, pray with urgency, when I say urgency, I mean pray like your life depends on it, because in many ways, it does!

When you start praying like this things will begin to change, you will see breakthroughs in areas where you have been stuck, you will see healing where there was sickness, you will see deliverance where there was been bondage and you will see doors opening that have been shut for years.

I challenge you today to step up your prayer game, do not settle for powerless Christianity, and do not be content with just getting by.

Press in for more of God's power!

Pray until the ground shakes beneath your feet!

Pray until the chains of bondage fall off!

Pray until you see the manifestation of God's glory in your life and in the lives of those around you!

And get set for stability, progress, and great achievements

CONCLUSION

Now that we are finally concluding these great revelations which the Lord has been releasing to your heart, I want to resound it again that it doesn't matter what you may have been going through or the difficult challenges you may have been encountering, as long as you are in synergization with the Lord, you will win in life, in destiny and in all that God has called ye to do, because he that is in you is greater than he that is in the world.

Do you remember Philippians 4:13 (KJV) which says, "I can do all things through Christ which strengtheneth me." This is God's assurance to you that there is no way you can be with Him and situations of life whether natural, physical, or spiritual will be able to stop your progress and achievements. Do not forget synergizing with God is not about cooperating with Him or doing things for Him, It's about becoming one with Him in purpose and power and about positioning your life for His grace, favor empowerment, and all dimensions of glory and blessing to flow.

Stop trying to live life by your strength, the bible already tells us that "by strength shall no man prevail" If you keep trying in your strength then you will keep failing and keep being defeated. But when you are synergized with God, you will never fail because you are not just living your life, you are living His life. You are not just doing your work; you are doing His work, and you are not just pursuing your dreams; you are fulfilling His divine purpose for your life. And let me tell ye, there is nothing more glorious, nothing more satisfying than this! And when ye do this, oh my! The results are extraordinary! You will begin to operate on a different level altogether because things that were once impossible become possible, obstacles become steppingstones and you begin to see with His eyes, think with His mind, and love with His heart.

I know God has richly blessed you and I know that God is set to bring you into greater levels of grace and breakthroughs in Jesus' mighty name amen.

A SPECIAL CALL TO SALVATION & NEW BEGINNINGS FROM APOSTLE DR. DAVID PHILEMON

Dear Beloved,
God loves you deeply and has brought you to this moment for a reason. No matter your past, His love and forgiveness are available to you.

The Bible says in John 3:16, "For God so loved the world that He gave His one and only Son, that whoever believes in Him shall not perish but have eternal life." Jesus Christ came to save you, offering you a new life of purpose and peace.

If you're ready to accept Jesus as your Lord and Savior, pray this simple prayer:

The Salvation Prayer

"Heavenly Father, I come to You in the Name of Jesus. I acknowledge that I am a sinner in need of a Savior. I believe that Jesus Christ is Your Son, that He died for my sins, and that You raised Him from the dead. I repent of my sins and turn to You with

my
Whole heart. Jesus, I ask You to come into my life. Be my Lord and my Savior. I surrender my life to You. Fill me with Your Holy Spirit, guide me on the path of righteousness, and help me to follow Your script for my life. Thank you, Father, for saving me. In the name of Jesus. Amen."

Welcome to the Family of God!

If you have just prayed this prayer, Congratulations! You are now a child of God, and heaven is rejoicing. Your journey has begun, and we're here to support you as you grow in faith and discover God's unique plans for you.

Next Steps:
• Connect with a Bible-believing church.
• Read the Bible Daily: God's Word is your guide.
• Pray Regularly: Prayer is your lifeline to God.
• Share Your Faith: Don't keep the good news to yourself.